Cut to the Chase 0.5

Cut to the Chase 0.5

Funny, challenging and straight talking for men

Lee and Baz

Authentic

MILTON KEYNES ● COLORADO SPRINGS ● HYDERABAD

15 14 13 12 11 10 09   7 6 5 4 3 2 1

First published 2009 by Authentic Media
9 Holdom Avenue, Bletchley, Milton Keynes, Bucks, MK1 1QR, UK
1820 Jet Stream Drive, Colorado Springs, CO 80921, USA
OM Authentic Media, Medchal Road, Jeedimetla Village, Secunderabad 500 055,
A.P., India
www.authenticmedia.co.uk

Authentic Media is a division of IBS-STL U.K., limited by guarantee, with its
Registered Office at Kingstown Broadway, Carlisle, Cumbria, CA3 0HA.
Registered in England & Wales No. 1216232. Registered charity 270162.

British Library Cataloguing in Publication Data
A catalogue record for this book is available from the British Library

ISBN 13: 978-1-86024-732-3

Cover design by David Smart
Print Management by Adare
Printed and bound in Great Britain by J.F. Print Ltd., Sparkford

This book is dedicated to Lee's Dad,
Peter Jackson (1939–2006) –
'a real man'

The Thankyous

From Baz

To all the men who have begun the journey of reality – no longer accepting that life with Jesus has to be boring and mundane but discovering that the Christian life is the most costly and challenging but the most rewarding. Keep on being determined to allow yourself to remove the mask of performance and letting the real self be seen, warts and all.

To all the men who have had a positive influence in my life over the last thirty-plus years, since I discovered there is a God who loves me and has time for me. Thanks for your patience, encouragement and belief in me. I really appreciate all that you have done.

To all the brilliant people at the Eccles Church, where I have the privilege of sharing their lives. You are a great bunch of people who inspire me to keep on being real with God, others and myself. Keep on pursuing God and his ways and don't settle for good but God.

To Linda, my best friend and wife. You have been, and are still, such a great encourager. Thanks for continuing to believe the best in me even when I am a typical man and such a pain in the backside. I love you and always will.

Finally, to God, who never gives up on me. He continues to amaze me by how he loves me and keeps encouraging me into a deeper friendship with him and to be more real and honest with him.

And from Lee

A big thanks to everyone who helped me write this book and has heard me harping on about it for years – especially people who have given us quotes and advice. Thanks for being so generous with your time. Special thanks go to Dave Roberts for the Japanese noodles in Leeds that started this all going.

Also, thanks to all the men I have met who have inspired me and kept me on the straight and narrow, and pushed me to dig in – especially Duncan, Lenny and, of course, Baz. Every time I meet you, you challenge me about my walk with God without even saying a word. I am really glad I met you and Linda.

Thanks, Mam, for everything . . .

And Dad, I miss you loads. You are still my greatest role model. Thanks for showing me that reality and faith are the best mix.

And lastly, to Clare, Lauren and Rhea – you have helped me so much. You see me every morning and still love me! Thank you.

visit us at www.leeandbaz.com

Contents

Foreword

OK, brace yourself.

The boys who wrote this book don't wear sandals. They probably haven't got any fishes on the rear end of their motors and, if they were to wear a tie, it would probably be looped around their heads. If you felt led to give them a Robin Reliant, they'd torch it.

Their book is just possibly about to scare the living daylights out of you. If you're looking for a warm, fuzzy, happy little book of 'precious-moments' encouragement that will exhort you to be a thoroughly nice Christian chap, put this epistle down right now! This book is raw, rude, offensive, gripping and occasionally gut-wrenching, with an honesty that will leave you breathless and a call that could seriously mess up your life – in the best possible way. Whether I agree with it all or endorse it totally as a chunk of print is a secret. But I do know these two kingdom thugs quite well. They are as sold out and committed to God as anyone you'll ever find. They've been through some rather tough stuff and still believe that there's a God (which is helpful). They don't just talk about *Braveheart* types, but are wildly passionate about waking men up to discover real masculinity.

Our culture has swallowed a troughful of trash when it comes to being a real man. Planet Chap is filled with blokes who have been drip-fed a consistently dull diet of junk about what it means to be authentically male. Perhaps that's why there's such a need for this brash alarm call. So I warmly welcome their contribution, and invite you to have your hair stand on end as you read it. Besides, the last book I read that was written specifically for men was called *Maximum Manhood* — sounds seriously intimidating to me . . .

Jeff Lucas

*Fantasy is what people want,
reality is what they need.*

Lauryn Hill

Introduction

Lee

Alex Buchanan came to preach at St Albans Vineyard Church in the UK a few years ago and said that he could judge the effectiveness of a church by seeing how many men there could 'wield a sword'. I thought about many of the Christian men I had known over the years and wondered how many of them would be able to pick up a sword, never mind wield it as if their life depended on it!

When I was at junior school in Billingham (in the north-east of England) I used to go after school to my Nanna Jackson's house, which wasn't very far away. I think my grandad was still working at the time. He was a shipyard worker and people say this is one of the hardest jobs you can do. I remember him coming in from work and undoing his boots on the kitchen stool. He just seemed a genuine man to me: he worked hard, his hands were rough, and often he looked tired and worn out, but there was something attractive about him simply because he was a 'real' man. I really looked up to him and enjoyed spending time with him. And to be honest, he had more masculinity than many of the people I have met who are supposedly 'living life to the full'. Sadly, he died before I became a teenager.

When I was a teenager I was at a theological college with my mam and dad, and I met a lot of interesting characters. Many of them were great, but my lasting impression is of tall, skinny, intellectual, nut-cutlet-eating vegetarians who didn't really have much relevance to society. Mr Bean in sandals, socks and a

Wallace and Gromit T-shirt is always an image that comes to mind. Then a friend of mine found this book called *Real Men Don't Eat Quiche* by Bruce Feirstein (who is a James Bond scriptwriter), and that kind of summed it up for me. Throughout my Christian experience as a teenager, every Christian event I went to provided candles and . . . a nice bit of quiche.

A predominantly middle-class church is probably seen in the same way as ballet − something for well-off people and not for real men.
Tony Watkins
of Damaris Trust commenting on the film *Billy Elliot*

This book is based partly around the deep theological truth that real men don't eat quiche! As I thought more about my childhood, I realized there were very few Christian men who actually inspired me. Why? I was attracted more to the 'realness' of non-Christian men as I grew up, and since then I have been seeking genuine male relationships in my life. And when I find them I know straight away . . .

I was once at a youth event as a DJ, and while getting some chips I started chatting to this guy called Ian. It was one of those conversations where you really start to connect with somebody. I realized that I had a lot in common with him, and saw that he was genuinely trying to live his life, fighting his way to Jesus. It was exciting for me because I hadn't met many people like that, especially in the North. (He lived on the South Coast for a while, and one of the reasons he moved there was to be in a church where he could have real relationships. He is now a missionary in Africa.) I meet him, Baz and a few other real men I respect, every year at a conference, where we have a great laugh together. And to be honest, it is one of the highlights of my year.

It was as Baz and I talked together that we realized that maybe we had something to say just by sharing our lives, and that is the reason for this book. It is not going to give you all the answers – you may agree with some things, you may disagree with others. Some things might wind you up and you might throw the book against the wall!

That's fine with us, so long as it sparks off some dialogue, some discussion, or gets some brain-matter moving, because we need to talk to each other, to let each other know about our hearts, our dreams, our visions. The big problem is that the Christian world thinks the pinnacle of Christian maleness is to be a 'nice bloke'.

But I am more attracted by someone like the couch potato Jim Royle from the TV series *The Royle Family*, or the seven-foot-one-inch Shaquille O'Neal who can dunk the ball hard in somebody's face, than I am by most Christian men I have met. I want to learn how to live my life, to harness my passions and my aggressions, to give everything I can in relationships, and hopefully, through some of this reality, actually start to stem the flow of men getting out of the church (or just as bad, those getting apathetic in the church!).

One of my basketball heroes is Vince Carter. He can fly to the hoop like no one I have ever seen before. He said (when asked about his similarity to the legend Michael Jordan), 'I just want to be Vince Carter.' It sounds simple but there is a lot in that. I simply want to be Lee Jackson, not to be put in a box and have my gifts caged up because they are not seen as relevant to church life. I want to shout and scream, I want to play basketball hard, I want to be known as a grafter, as someone who doesn't give up, as a good DJ, a good dad, a good husband, ultimately a good follower of Jesus.

If you spend your life in Christian culture and are not too careful, your real self, your true masculinity, can disappear – or certainly, it will be implied that it is not important.

Some say that Christian blokes no longer even know what it means to be masculine.

I was asked to do a men's day for a church in Yorkshire, and as I shared my heart for a couple of sessions, the men there genuinely responded. At the end, a 20-year-old lad came up to me and said, 'I just want to thank you for being real with me. I have been in the church for years and that is the first time someone has spoken to me and not talked down to me. You made it make sense!'

I was shocked that this lad had had to wait so long for a man to speak his language, and we wonder where all the men are . . . They have legged it – as simple as that!

As this book is about getting real with each other, a starter for ten . . . here's me getting real with you . . .

I was in the waiting room with all the other men, embarrassed to be there. We all giggled nervously and a few told forced jokes to help ease their nerves. But mainly it was silent, everyone realizing they were putting their manhood on the line – literally. One flinch from the scalpel and it would all be over! All our clothes and status had disappeared as soon as we put on those starched hospital gowns that always open when you don't want them to! Everyone was nervous, most had come with friends or partners, and the bloke opposite me was holding his wife's hand tightly.

The surgeon came out and started to explain the operation to us in friendly but graphic detail. Then I had the feeling I dread and, before I knew it, a male nurse was bringing me round as I was slouched on Clare's knee! I realized that my brief exit from the world had broken the ice among these macho men; they were all genuinely concerned for me, asking if I was all right and maybe starting to wonder whether I knew something they didn't! In that brief moment of concern I saw something of the real men, and not the 'me, my castle, my car, my job and my barbecue' men we all pretend to be. This book is a cry from the heart for genuine masculinity to rise up in the church and the nation.

The chapters are deliberately short and packed full of quotes and information, as well as true stories about things we have gone through. It is designed to be a description of real lives rather than in-depth theoretical theology. In the process of writing this book we contacted loads of people we know and asked them for a few comments they might want to share with other men. Some of them were happy for the chance to let off a bit of steam and open their hearts, and their comments are interspersed throughout. We give you first names in most cases, but you'll have to guess their second names!

Me and Baz are both followers of Jesus, and obviously this book reflects that, but I do know that most of this book is relevant to men in general and not just Christian blokes. Feel free to use it at your men's curry nights – just send us a curry as a thankyou.

If this book does nothing other than encourage you to be real with other men, then it has served its purpose. Enjoy . . .

The best we can find in our travels is an honest friend.

Robert Louis Stevenson (1850–94)

1

The Three Rs

Lee

This was the first chapter in Dead Men Walking *and we have left it at the beginning here too because this is the foundation the book is written from. This was, for me, where our roller-coaster journey started. Enjoy the ride . . .*

After I had spent three years as the only schools worker in Leeds, the organization I worked for — Leeds Faith in Schools — eventually had enough money to employ a second worker. This was very exciting for me, as I felt like the Lone Ranger some days! When the applications came in, we sifted through them in the normal way, except for one application. It was not on the typed form like all the others; it was a colourful, creative CV with photos and info crammed into its photocopied pages. As I glanced through it, there was a phrase that stuck out and persuaded me that we had found our next worker. It said: 'All youth work is based on the three Rs . . . Relationships, Relationships, Relationships.'

What a statement! I later found out that it had been written in the middle of the night in a haze of caffeine, but aren't a lot of good things? (Whether or not it's an original thought is difficult to tell, of course; and yes, it does lean towards the cheesy, but still . . .) The three Rs are not only applicable to youth work but to the whole of our lives.

Think about it — what is more important than relationships? Our relationships with our wife or girlfriend, children, family and friends are the most important things in our lives. Then there is our relationship with God: even if we don't follow him we still have a relationship with him. God is 'three in one', so even at the heart of God relationships are key. When Jesus came to earth, he spent his time with a few rough men and women, trying to build relationships with them and make a difference in their lives. He could have chosen to ride on a cloud or live as a hermit – you can choose to be anything if you are God, I guess!

The evangelist J. John spoke at a young evangelists' conference I was invited to. I can't remember much of what he said, except for one of his now-famous phrases: 'The main thing is to keep the main thing the main thing!' The main thing for us is relationships. Nothing is more important, and nothing comes close to matching it. The whole of this book is based on this simple piece of common sense. Putting relationships first in our lives means that everything else falls into its rightful place. Let's face it – all men think they have healthy relationships, but how many of us really do?

Even some of the new men's resources out there talk about being a man (*Grrrr*, like Tony the Tiger), but sometimes they forget that while we need manly stuff, we also need to be challenged about our relationships. I think there is a healthy balance to be found – we need typical manly-type activities combined with a challenge about our view of others/God. It seems that Jesus did that with his disciples: a bout of fishing, a good meal and a tough question – 'Who do you say I am?'

Honesty

To move towards deeper relationships with people, we need to develop a greater sense of honesty and realness. I used to work at the Crown Court in Leeds (I thought I'd start as a criminal and work my way up!). As an admin officer, I shuffled paper from one side of my desk to the other and then went home. In the mornings there used to be a ritual that drove me mad: it was the 'say hello to everyone' game. Everyone used to say, 'Hello, good morning, how are you?' but no one ever replied honestly or ever listened for a reply! 'Yeah, fine thanks', 'Not bad' or 'Fair to middling' were the only responses. Some people even answered the question when you hadn't asked them!

I loved giving people more information than they wanted: 'Well, I feel a bit tired, actually, and I'm concerned about my relationship with my wife, and my dog has fleas.' You have never seen people run so fast. We need to get real with each other and stop covering over the cracks with our English barriers. I must admit, though, there is a fine line between being honest and becoming a constant whinger. We will have to find the balance somewhere.

Football was invented because men have got
nothing to say to their mates.
Ben Elton[1]

For men, the depth issue is easy to push further — try steering conversations away from football, cars and 'what I would do if I won the lottery', and see what happens. Beyond the banter and football talk there is often a man who is lonely and craves true friendship. I know that from my own life. I still have feelings of loneliness and these feelings are shared by some of my (honest) friends. Is the Internet so popular with men because you only share the bits you want to share in selective Facebook-type relationships?

Purpose-driven relationships?

I have no doubt as to the validity of such relationships, but we have to balance things up. Can we deliberately spend time with people for no reason other than to spend time with them? As someone who enjoys networking, it is difficult not to talk about work all the time, but when I don't, it often feels great just to connect with someone. As we understand one another more, God makes the right connections anyway – so, bonus! A while back my friend Simon said to me, 'Let's get together, Lee; I feel as if we're drifting apart.' We had both been busy and he was right – we needed time together, not just for the sake of our work but just for our own sakes.

Christian churches of all kinds, of course, major on 'preaching up' commitment – to our marriages, to our friendships, to Christ and (by no means least) commitment to those churches . . . Nevertheless, the fact remains that, in the cultural climate of the West, our commitment to one another is very low indeed.
Meic Pearse and Chris Matthews[2]

An influential youth leader once 'announced' to me that he had chosen me as his friend – we had a couple of meals together and now he only talks to me when he needs something! Mmmm. Since God has pressed on me the importance of relationships with others, I have spent time writing more emails and my phone bill has gone up. So it is not without its costs, but the results are worth it. I used to coach and play basketball in school and I spent a considerable time with one group of sixth formers who formed a team, playing basketball with them, organizing trips, breaking up fights at their parties and just hanging out with them over the summer holidays. Now they have left school, they still keep in touch and invite me to the occasional party, which is great. All the time I spent getting them back together and checking if they were all right has paid off with, I hope, friendships for many years to come. No, they are not all Christians, but I have a special friendship with some of them and they are not embarrassed to be seen with 'that bloke who did my assemblies'.

Fragrance

But what happens if people don't like you?[3] I used to be in a basketball team where most of the members seemed to hate me. I left in the end because of it. I had helped them, been a faithful member of the team but, for whatever reason, they just hated me. They loved it when I missed a shot or got fouled – it was weird. I went back after I had left to play against them and they still heckled me and were delighted when we lost the match. Some people you will never connect with. I can get on with most people,[4] but these guys simply hated me. Then I read a bit from the Bible that freaked me out:

> Through us, he brings knowledge of Christ. Everywhere we go, people breathe in the exquisite fragrance. Because of Christ, we give off a sweet scent rising to God, which is recognized by those on the way of salvation – an aroma redolent with life. But those on the way to destruction treat us more like the stench from a rotting corpse.
>
> This is a terrific responsibility. Is anyone competent to take it on? No – but at least we don't take God's Word, water it down, and then take it to the streets to sell it cheap. We stand in Christ's presence when we speak; God looks us in the face. We get what we say straight from God and say it as honestly as we can.
>
> Does it sound like we're patting ourselves on the back, insisting on our credentials, asserting our authority? Well, we're not. Neither do we need letters of endorsement, either to you or from you. You yourselves are all the endorsement we need. Your very lives are a letter that anyone can read by just looking at you. Christ himself wrote it – not with ink, but with God's living Spirit; not chiseled into stone, but carved into human lives – and we publish it.
>
> 2 Corinthians 2:14 – 3:3, *The Message*

Maybe I was the smell of death to these blokes. These verses have stayed with me as a reminder of what a responsibility we have to try to maintain good relationships with people, but sometimes you just have to shake the dust from your feet and move on. However, I do believe this is a last and not a first response, as some people seem to think. I have been a 'sweet smell' to some people though, you will be glad to know. I used to buy a sandwich on the way to work every Friday, and one day the shop owner said she was selling up the business and moving to France. We had always had a laugh together and I was sad to see her go. On the last day I gave her a hug and wished her well and, to my amazement, she said that there was 'something different' about me and she had always enjoyed serving me. Obviously, the way I ordered sandwiches was somehow different to other people's sandwich orders! The fragrance of Christ again? Who knows.

Carry on loving

I am a big comedy fan and I love some of the old Ealing comedies and the early *Carry On* films. But amazingly, many of those comedians were paranoid, mean, self-destructive and lonely people. How people who are so gifted manage to destroy the people around them I will never understand. In all the biographies and documentaries of comedians, there are only one or two who are always talked of very highly. Hattie Jacques (the ward matron in the *Carry On* films) is one of these people. She was a true friend to the greatest collection of outcasts in film history – the *Carry On* cast. I may not be seen as a 'success' in many people's eyes. But I genuinely hope people will talk about me as a person who cared about relationships and not just a man who achieved a lot at the expense of others.

*Many men's meetings I've been to are about as
relational as a GP's waiting room.*
Anonymous

Relational church?

The emergence in recent years of new forms of church is very exciting, and I desperately want these to work, especially for men, as it is probably our last hope of truly reaching a lost people group. Once you get a taste of genuine relationships in and out of church life, there is no going back. Anonymous meetings and shallow friendships stick out like a sore thumb when you have seen and experienced glimpses of the real thing.

Get real

- Arrange a meeting with someone you work with, for no reason other than to talk to them.
- Try to answer more honestly when someone you know asks you how you are.
- When you ask people how they are, wait to hear an answer.
- Get a cheap phone-call package and make that call you keep putting off.
- When you are 'filling up' your diary, remember the three Rs.
- Talk to your not-yet-Christian friends about your weaknesses as well, so they know you are not superhuman and you want a real relationship with them.
- If the previous point does not apply to you, then get some not-yet-Christian friends!

Character is much easier kept than recovered.

Thomas Paine (1737–1809)

2

Don't Go Breaking My Heart

Baz

*A heart softened by God is a heart
that will beat in time with God's.*

After leaving Bible college in 1985, I went to live and work in Sheffield. A friend of mine worked for the YMCA as their Christian Outreach worker, and as part of my course at college I had done a week of schools work with him. At the end of the week he had asked me to consider working with him voluntarily following my course. So that is what I did. I lived at the YMCA, which was an education in itself, and worked in schools and helped with youth services, weekends and other events.

Bad news

My mother is one of those ladies who will only contact me if I am in trouble or something has happened that I need to know about. One morning I was informed that there was a telephone call for me at the reception desk. I picked the phone up and the conversation went as follows:

'Hello?'

'Barrie, it's your mother.'

(Now, you need to know that no one calls me Barrie except my mother, and that's usually only when I'm in trouble.)

'Hi, Mam. How are you?'

'I've got some news for you. Your gran is dead. Bye.'

That was it – the phone line was dead and so was my gran. All those classes my mother had been to at the hospital on 'how to break bad news sensitively' had really come into their own that morning!

I stood there feeling numb. Tears began flowing down my cheeks as I thought about the fact that I would never see my gran again.

One of the receptionists became aware of me just standing there crying, so she asked me if there was anything wrong.

I felt like saying, 'Oh no, I often do this on a morning before I go and take a lesson.' She was genuinely concerned, but I just blurted out, 'My gran has died!' and went to my room.

I sat in my room distraught. The lady I had lived with for many years and who had looked after me like a mother had gone, and I had not had the chance to see her one final time. There were so many things I wanted to say to her, like thanks for being there and putting up with me and my moods, and anger at times. I wanted to tell her I loved her. I knew she had loved me by the way she looked after me. We have never been good as a family at telling one another that we love each other.

I sat there wishing I could have one more chance to tell her, but that was not going to happen. Suddenly there was a knock on my door, and as I opened it, I saw my mate Steve standing there with two cups of tea. What would we do without tea at times of trouble? Steve sat with me as I prattled on about everything and nothing, and even in the silence it was good to know someone was there to empathize with me.

Three days later I got another phone call from my mother. She was probably ringing to give me the details of the funeral, I thought. How wrong I was!

The call went like this:

'Barrie, it's your mother.'

'Hi, Mam.'

'I've got some more news for you.'

I thought, *Not more bad news!*

'What?' I asked.

'Your gran, she's not dead.'

'What do you mean, she's not dead?!'

'I made a mistake – it's her next-door neighbour, Olive, who's dead. Bye.'

Once again the line was dead. But this time Gran was alive and kicking and Olive was dead! I could not believe what I was hearing – apparently someone had told my mother that my gran had died, and then she found out three days later that she was alive. Where have we heard that story before?

I was running around the YMCA building crying and shouting, 'She's not dead, she's alive!' People were looking at me as if I was mad. When people heard the story they were pleased for me, but they were in hysterics over how my mother had informed me both times of the news. I was ecstatic that my gran was alive and I would have the chance to see her again and tell her I loved her.

When you love someone and you discover they have died, your emotions are pulled all over the place – even more so when you know that they have died without knowing Jesus personally. My gran was brought up with ten brothers and sisters in quite a religious family. When she discovered I had become a Christian, she said the following to me in quite a stern tone: 'That Christianity might be OK for you, but don't try to get me into it. I want nothing to do with it, so don't bother talking to me about it.'

I found out some time later that she had been put off Christianity by her parents, who had made their children read the Bible every Sunday afternoon. I think one of her brothers didn't help the cause either.

I loved my gran and I had been given another chance to pray for her salvation, but also talk to her personally about

Jesus. I knew that all the years I had lived with my gran
and grandad, I had taken them for granted and sometimes
abused the love they showed me. My grandad had died in the
seventies. He had a painful death due to cancer. I remember
standing outside his bedroom door one night, listening to him
crying out to God, 'Please take me, as I cannot bear the pain
any more!'

When you love someone, you want the best for them.
If they are not Christians, you are desperate for them to
discover God's love. If you're not, I would suggest you don't
love them enough.

Real love

In John's Gospel chapter 11, we see what real love is. Jesus
has heard that his close friend Lazarus has died and is quite
calm about the whole situation. Eventually he is moved by
the weeping of Mary and her friends over Lazarus's death.
We read: 'When Jesus saw her weeping, and the Jews who
had come along with her also weeping, he was deeply moved
in spirit and troubled' (John 11:33). Verse 35 is the shortest
verse in the Bible: 'Jesus wept.'

Why did he weep? Because he had compassion for the
people and he loved Lazarus. This doesn't mean a few tears
down the face and quickly wipe them away before anyone sees
you showing some emotion! But he *wept*, probably making a
scene but not bothered about what people thought, as he was
deeply moved by what was going on.

If this kind of compassion was to engulf each Christian man,
young and old, in this country, we would soon have a revival
of people coming to know Christ. Until we are willing to let
God break our hearts with his love and compassion for the
people of this nation and others, we will never reach out to
people to share the good news of Jesus.

The other day I was shocked as I read about a young boy being murdered and torched to death, and also an elderly man who lived locally being beaten to death. What shocked me was how unmoved by these stories I was. I just pushed it aside with some thought of how society is getting worse. It is easy to get so consumed by our everyday commitments that we lose the rhythm of God's heartbeat for our neighbours, school, college, university friends, work colleagues, family, friends and the different people we come across daily.

Why is this? Is it because we have lost the first love of God in our own lives? Is it because we are no longer concerned about people dying without knowing God personally for themselves? Have we given up sharing our faith because we have lost confidence in the gospel, the good news of Jesus? Or is it simply because our hearts have become hard to the hurting, needy people in our society and world?

Some years ago, I was encouraged to pray the following prayer: 'God, will you give me the heart of Jesus, so I will feel as he feels for people? Will you give me the eyes of Jesus, so I will see as he does for people? Will you give me the mind of Jesus, so that I will think as he does about people? Will you give me the mouth of Jesus, so I will speak as he does to people? Will you give me the ears of Jesus, so I will listen as he does to people?'

When I have said this prayer sincerely, I have been amazed at the outcome. My heart at times becomes heavy with pain as I listen to or talk with people about what is going on in their lives. I have started to see people in a different light; not through my own eyes of judgement but through eyes that really feel love and acceptance towards them. I want to reach out and be there for them in whatever way God sees fit.

Living this way is exciting and rewarding: letting God get hold of you and take you on the great rollercoaster journey of fun, laughter and tears which we call life, rubbing shoulders with those he has put in your path to make a difference in their lives and even introduce them to this living God. It's far better than allowing your heart to get hard and cold, becoming one of those people who just used to get excited about sharing their faith.

A few months after I had that really interesting phone call from my mother, I received another which went like this:

'Barrie, it's your mother. Your gran is in hospital; she's not very well.'

'What's wrong with her, Mam?'

'She's dying.'

'Are you sure?'

'Yes, I saw her today. She's in ward B4. Bye.'

Fortunately, after the earlier phone-call fiasco, I had been to Darlington a few times to visit my gran. So even though I was upset by the news, I had had the chance to see her. I phoned the hospital to see if I could arrange a time with them to see my gran outside visiting time. The reason for this was to avoid bumping into my father. He was my biological father – and that was it. He had lived in another country most of my life, and hated the sight of me – especially since I had become a Christian – probably because of some of the things he was involved with.

The hospital agreed to allow me some time in the evening after visiting hours to see my gran. I got the train up to Darlington and went to see my mother and brother in the daytime. In the evening I walked to the hospital, feeling very apprehensive about what I was going to see. My mother had pre-warned me that my gran had lost a lot of weight and had limited eyesight.

Hospitals are not my favourite places, and I have been known to faint at just the smell when I walk through the main doors! When I worked for a Methodist church in Northern Ireland I had to do hospital visits, and many times I came out ready to puke or faint.

I managed to pull myself together and get to the ward. The nurse informed me that Gran was asleep and I had fifteen minutes. I approached the bed cautiously and fearfully. There she was asleep, like a skeleton, so helpless and lifeless. This was not the lady who had worked so hard running her own bakery shop, or the lady who used to make the most fantastic sausage stew or Christmas cake. The lady who had such a distinguished laugh was not laughing any more. My gran was an amazing woman with whom I lived for many years during my childhood and later teens. I sat quietly looking at her frail body, thinking what a wonderful woman she was, when all of a sudden she woke.

'Gran! How are you?'

You stupid idiot – she's dying! I thought.

Then she called out, 'Who's that?'

'It's Barrie,' I replied.

What she said next still brings a smile to my face.

'Nick?'

'No, Barrie.'

'Joe?'

'No, Barrie.'

'Buck?'

'No, Barrie.'

'John?'

'No, Barrie.'

This went on for some time as she went through the list of her brothers, sons and grandchildren, and finally got to me. I asked her if she had had many visitors. She informed me that she hadn't, while constantly calling me by other people's names (no doubt the names of the many people who had visited her!).

What I was to hear next caused me to ask my gran to repeat what she had just said.

'I have had this man at the end of my bed who just kept saying to me, "Sarah, come to me. I love you." He stands there with his arms open wide, smiling at me, urging me to come with him. Do you know who he could be?'

By then I was crying uncontrollably. 'It's Jesus, Gran!'

'What does he want with me?' she asked.

'He wants you to be with him.'

I went on to explain the gospel to my gran and told her how she could have assurance of eternal life before she died.

She said she was going to pray and ask God to forgive her and ask Christ into her life. Immediately after that she stopped talking. Initially I thought she had died, so I leant over and listened. I could hear the faintest of breathing. I held her hand and prayed for her and then leant over and kissed her goodbye. I knew I would not see her again this side of eternity.

I left the hospital very emotional but grateful to God for that last time with my gran and for what he had done in her life while she had been in hospital. God had heard my prayers for my gran. I had asked specifically to have an opportunity to share with her about Jesus, and he had come through big time!

I ran and danced around the hospital car park, thanking God and shouting at Satan – telling him he had lost another battle to the Outrageous Grace of God. Tears streamed down my face as I experienced a combination of joy and sadness, knowing my gran was about to begin a brand-new life with Jesus at the end of her own.

At her funeral I listened to the local vicar as he informed the mourners of the change in this lady's life in her last three weeks. As I smiled within, he commented on my gran's desire to pray, have the Bible read to her and take communion with him. I knew one day I would see Sarah McIntyre again, as this was just the beginning of her life at the grand age of eighty-nine.

During my visits to different churches to speak or participate in youth weekends, I come across many people who struggle with sharing their faith. The main struggle is with guilt; the guilt of not doing it or failing at it.

I believe this is often due to the way people are being discipled about evangelism. If we could get over to people that God wants to use us in sharing our faith in a natural and relevant way (where we remain emotionally honest), we would see a dramatic shift in the way people behave when opportunities come their way.

One of the biggest obstacles for men in sharing their faith today, I believe, is all to do with identity. A visiting speaker at my church, who was doing a three-week series on 'The Fatherhood of God', said: 'If you grasp your true identity in God – that you are a Prince, a Son of God – this will affect every other area of your life.'

He went on to say: 'As you allow your relationship with your Heavenly Father to improve, your worship, prayer, Bible reading, witness, work and family life will all improve.'

We need to understand that if we can experience this in our hearts, it will transform our endeavours. As Christian men today, we need to have our hearts broken by the Holy Spirit so we will weep like Jesus did. Why? Because we will then see people and treat them as God wants us to. No longer will we be immune to the horrendous things we witness on the news or read in the papers, but we will actually be provoked to do something!

It's about time we men became real men, unafraid of emotions and prepared to carry godly burdens rather than our worldly ones. Such an experience might mean we will cry as never before or hurt with a pain in our hearts as never before. Good! This is how God feels daily for his people, his world. Isn't it about time we had more of this within the church – but more importantly, outside it, where it really counts?

How's your heart today?

Questions

- When was the last time your heart was really broken by God?
- Is your identity placed in God your Father or in your reputation?
- Do you want to have the heart of God for people?
- Are you willing to let him break your heart, no matter what the cost?
- On a scale of 1 to 10, how would you rate yourself in the whole area of compassion?
- Are you really bothered that people are dying without Jesus? If not, why not?

Faith goes out through the window when beauty comes in through the door.

George Edward Moore (1873–1958)

3

Braveheart

Matt Page

Even though this chapter may sound a little dated now because of the 1990s film reference, it was a key in the journey me and Baz have been on and still has lots of relevance today — especially since the nice, 'don't offend anyone ever'-type attitude is still the mainstream in many churches and, dare I say it, even in men's meetings.

> *You can't escape it — there is something wild in the heart of every man.*
> John Eldredge[5]

I was at the UK Pioneer Leaders' Conference in 1997. It was a great conference, and I don't say that too often! I spent time with my friends and did a couple of mad things to keep boredom from the door. Behind the conference stage were fifteen-feet-high polystyrene letters spelling out 'R-E-V-I-V-A-L'. This was too good an opportunity for me to miss. So one night, when everyone had gone to bed (the Christian time being about 10 p.m.), we moved the letters around and put some on top of each other so that it spelt 'V-E-R-A'. The best thing was that Gerald Coates, the Pioneer team leader, thought it was a well-known practical joker who had done it, and he went through an elaborate twenty-minute fake trial and conviction of this completely innocent man, who was carried out of the auditorium by six big lads. I feel better now confessing that to you lot!

'Come on!'

That conference was amazing. I remember pushing through with God in a few unusual ways and also just having a good laugh with him. We had times of ministry that were great fun and very meaningful to a lot of people. Apart from the practical jokes, that conference had an amazing effect on my life. During one of the meetings, a group of men from River Church (Maidstone, UK) came onto the stage with a four-foot sword from the film *Braveheart*. They explained how the film had affected them as they had studied it as a church and a youth group. That night was the first time I heard the famous prayer cry of 'COME ON!', which is now a familiar thing – people have even preached on it. These guys shared their hearts about *Braveheart*, and then they just screamed at the tops of their voices and went into a real war cry. It stirred something up in me that night and I knew I would never be the same again. And when I watched the film, God spoke to me about passion, aggression and prayer. No other film has ever affected me so much.

Martin Scott writes:

> We must press beyond the realm of theory and beyond simply discovering 'good practice' to an encounter with the Lord who trains us for war (Judg. 3:10; Ps. 144:1). There is an anointing that we can receive from him that will break the passivity within us and get us ready for war (Joel 2:11; 3:9–16). He is looking for a fight! . . . It is important, as we press in on God, that we are not simply warfare orientated. Worship of Jesus is the highest call, yet worship and warfare are not in opposition, for in Psalm 149 we see that the expression of warfare was birthed in the place of intimacy.[6]

It appears to me that the film industry has changed over the last few years and *Braveheart* was definitely a result of that. Traditionally, most male action characters have been plain macho with bad attitudes to women and anyone else. It is hard to connect with them and you even feel sorry for them. James Bond is the obvious example of this, although he does seem to be getting better with age. He gathers gadgets, kills the baddies and makes love to innumerable women who submit to his charms (and his diseases!) and bow to his superior masculinity. Thank God for the Judi Dench character 'M' (Bond's boss), who managed to be feminine, strong and certainly wouldn't end up in bed with him! Since *Braveheart*, of course, there have been other films, like *Gladiator* and *Fight Club*, that could also be studied in this way.

It's not just that a man needs a battle to fight,
he needs someone to fight for.
John Eldredge[7]

Braveheart is a film of warfare and relationships. It created a stir among film fans, and it has also rekindled something of Scottish nationalism in both a positive and negative way. There are *Braveheart* websites, message boards, fan clubs, and even talk of a *Braveheart* conference where different people could come to explain how the film has affected their lives. If that happens, I would love to share how God spoke to me through this film, which may be a bit of a surprise to some in the Scottish National Party.

A sword for the Lord

Once I had seen the sword that the guys from River Church had brought, I just knew I had to have one. It was a hand-and-a-half sword, which was very heavy and definitely the real thing! Someone must have overheard me saying how much I wanted this sword, because an envelope arrived through my door containing £125 in cash, which was the right amount for it, and a note which said, 'A sword for the Lord and for Gideon' (Judg. 7:20).

We have no great war; our great war is a spiritual war.
From the film *Fight Club*[8]

It certainly causes a few reactions when I walk into a conference or meeting with a four-foot sword! When I pray for people with my sword, it has been amazing – and it definitely keeps their attention! I prayed with a senior church leader once at a conference and put the sword into his hands as he kept his eyes closed. As he opened his eyes after we had prayed for a while, he was amazed to see this sword in his hand. He had bought himself a *Braveheart* poster to go above his desk, had seen visions of the sword and just knew it was right for him to pick it up and to use it to pray with.

I also prayed with a Scandinavian guy once who was about six foot five. As I prayed for him, he fell backwards onto the sword, which was wedged on a chair. It started to bend, but I just managed to pull it free before it snapped and severed his spine! More prayer meetings like that, please.

Don't take my word for it. Why not dig into the film and let God speak to you through it? Here are some study notes on *Braveheart* which you can either use yourself, or use as a group after watching the film. These notes have been used by River Church in leadership training.

Braveheart study notes

1. What does the story of the film tell us about Wallace?

- He had a period of training.

- He was recognized as a leader by his peers.
- He didn't cling to 'privileges'.
- He was not interested in committees.
- He was prepared to die for what he believed in.
- No compromise.
- Honesty.
- He was aggressive, even wild.
- Prophetic? (He said, 'I see strength in you . . . ' to the Queen.)
- Strategic – not just raw aggression.
- Pushed others out (e.g. Robert the Bruce).
- Happy to get behind others.
- He died and others took on the battle.

2. What was Jesus like and can we see these qualities in the film?

- A man who lost the comforts of home.
- Came into a lifestyle that was alien to him.
- Didn't crave recognition – was totally secure.
- Didn't just talk – used action.
- No compromise.
- Didn't cling to privileges.
- Rejected the institutions of the day.
- Was honest.
- Was aggressive, even wild.
- Called a radical.
- Upset the political stability of the day.
- Was totally subversive.
- Prophetic.
- Trained others up.
- Died for a principle – freedom for the world.

3. In the following quote from the screenwriter Randall Wallace, try substituting the word 'film' with 'gospel'

Every tale has a message; in what it elevates or attacks, in what it uplifts or denies, every story makes its point. This film stands upon the affirmations of honour and courage, of faithfulness to the promises of the heart. It is a story built on the history of a man who served these values more than himself, and whose life confronts us with the belief that to put such things above life is life itself. The making of *Braveheart* has been an act of devotion. Those who have served the soul of this film have, I think, been changed by it. When we have felt unable and unworthy of the attempt to tell such a story, it has made our hearts brave enough to try.

4. Now read Isaiah 53.

5. What does it take to be a William Wallace?

- Discipline
- Cost/sacrifice
- Servanthood
- Discipleship
- Endurance
- Strategy
- Passion
- Aggression/power

6. Can you think of any more parallels between Wallace and Jesus than are mentioned here?

7. What does the film teach us about the following things?

- The real heart of a man
- Church life
- Living
- Dying

- Destiny
- Our jobs
- Family

8. Also check out 2 Samuel 23:8–12. Are there any parallels with William Wallace there?

I'd stay away from ecstasy. This is a drug so powerful, it makes white people think they can dance.

Lenny Henry[9]

4

Fantasy Island

Matt Page

Fantasy was the way I tried to escape from the reality of life. Escapism is the fear that stops you and me facing up to what is really going on in our lives.

In the 1980s there was a TV programme called *Fantasy Island*. Each week people from all walks of life would fly to an exotic island and have their fantasies fulfilled. The owner of the island was like a modern version of Father Christmas or an American version of Jimmy Savile in *Jim'll Fix It*. He would be informed of the arrival of these people by his faithful colleague, Tattoo, who would go running to him, shouting as he pointed to the sky, 'Boss, Boss, de plane!'

People's fantasies varied from meeting a long-lost love or doing something for the last time before they died, to having the chance to re-live a day and rectify a mistake or regret. Each week you knew people were going to leave the island satisfied, as they had fulfilled their fantasy. If it were that easy to have our fantasies fulfilled, a lot more men would get themselves into trouble and mess up their lives and other people's. William A. Orton once said, 'If you keep your mind sufficiently open, people will throw a lot of rubbish into it.' How true this is. Each day we are bombarded with information by the media, which, if we are not careful, can have us sliding down the hill of fantasy and lustful desires.

Masturbation

Unfortunately, as a young boy, I got into masturbation far too early. I say 'unfortunately' not because masturbation in itself is wrong, but because it got me opening my mind to all sorts of fantasy. It all started when I was about ten years old. One day, as I met some friends in the local fields to play, I was presented with the question, 'Have you had your first wank yet?' I had no idea what they were on about, which they probably guessed by the look of puzzlement on my face. So they took me into some bushes and showed me what they meant. After they had done it to themselves, they informed me it was my turn.

I felt scared and embarrassed and did not want to continue this sex-education lesson. However, it was made very clear to me that if I didn't, I could no longer be part of their gang — they were about five years older than me and I loved knocking around with them. When I got home I felt very confused. I was excited by the sensation I had just experienced, but the circumstances in which it had happened made me feel angry, upset and full of hatred.

I did, however, continue to masturbate at home in the luxury and privacy of my bedroom. I was determined to become a man. I was going for the world record. If there had been an event at the Olympics, I certainly would have represented Great Britain and probably would have won the gold medal! I tell you this not to shock or embarrass anyone but to show that most men get into this through discovery with their peers rather than their parents telling them about it; which, for a lot of men when they later become Christians, creates feelings of embarrassment, guilt and dirtiness.

As a teenager you knew you were not the only person masturbating. Most of us have gone through the phase of fantasizing about the latest sexy TV or film star, or the girl at school we fancied, or our mate's mother or our school teacher.

I can relate to Jonathan Ross when he said to Britt Eckland at a Comedy Awards, 'Can I thank you for helping me to get through my difficult years.' At the age of 17, when I became a Christian, I was still trying to get into the *Guinness Book of Records*. Gradually, through prayer, reading the Bible, attending church and being involved with other Christians, God began to make me aware of sin in my life: stealing, jealousy, hatred, anger, lust, and numerous other things. I started to become aware that sin was messing up the person God wanted me to be, as well as my relationship with him.

In the Christian world there are different views on the subject of masturbation. Some people will tell you it is a sin, and others will tell you to put it under the cold tap, or that you need to be more disciplined. Usually none of these men own up to the fact that they once struggled or are still struggling with it.

Before Linda and I were married, we were at church together one day, and she was leading worship while I was there as part of the congregation. At the end of the meeting an opportunity was given for people to receive prayer. Quite a lot of people responded to this. One of the leaders of the church asked if I would pray for a young man in the worship team who had acknowledged he would like prayer.

So I went up to this guy and offered to pray for him. After about five minutes' silence he plucked up enough courage to inform me what he wanted prayer for. Yes, you've guessed it: masturbation. I now knew I had a decision to make – to pretend to be holy and nod my head in a spiritual way, or be honest and tell him I was struggling as well. I chose the latter and said to him, 'Great. You pray for me and I'll pray for you.' Before we even began, you could see that he was already feeling better. Was this down to the fact that he didn't feel judged or condemned, and someone knew the struggles he was going through?

Fantasies

In the 1980s a well-known church leader, speaker and author offended a lot of other Christian leaders by his remarks on masturbation. He said something like: 'It's not a sin to masturbate, but I have not met anyone who does not sin while masturbating.' What he was implying was that to get aroused, you have to let your mind enter fantasy island, which then leads to sin. Because of this, some Christian leaders refused to be on the same platform as him, even though most of them would have done exactly what this man implied at some time in their lives, and probably as Christians.

Masturbation can and does become habitual in any man's life if he keeps feeding his sexual fantasies. 'Don't knock masturbation. It's sex with someone I love.'[10] This is very funny, but it's not true. Yes, you may love your willy, but with you and your willy are the sordid thoughts that accompany the act of masturbation.

We do not read in the Bible, 'Thou shalt not masturbate', so what is God's view? Does this mean it's not an issue with him or that it's OK to do it? I read a Christian magazine recently whose entire edition was dedicated to exploring the issue of sex. There was a section entitled 'Should we scratch the itch?'

So where does masturbation fit into the arena? Many people both single and married find sexual release in this practice. When you have no partner, your sex drive still goes on. But it's vital to manage it correctly – whether you're married or not. Just like physical hunger, your sex drive needs the right nutrition – not junk food like pornography or fantasies. So if you are married: wish your partner were with you. If you are single: 'scratch the itch'. But be careful of over indulgence. We do need to be able to discuss the issue of masturbation. In the past we have been either silent and embarrassed, or heavy and condemning. There is no actual teaching in the Bible on masturbation, but there are clear directives concerning other sexual practices. Concerning masturbation it would seem that God leaves it to the individual to decide what's right for him or her.[11]

This was a very interesting and challenging article, which surely raised some eyebrows, and no doubt will cause a few feathers to be stirred even now as you read it! I am not knocking masturbation for the sake of it, but I am challenging the way we allow our minds to be filled with things that are not conducive to our Christian walk or our future lives, whether we plan to be single or married. If we plan to marry in the future, or if we are already married, the enemy will try to use the things we store up in our minds to bring division between ourselves and our partner.

Older women

When I was about 16 I had one fantasy that ruled my thought-life nearly every day. This was to be seduced by an adult lady. I thought that if I could sleep with an older woman, she would be able to teach me how to make love to women so that I would not feel like a novice. On two occasions women older than me have made a pass at me. The first was when I was 16 and working as an apprentice central heating engineer. The lady whose house we were working in started to come on to me. Even though I had dreamt about such a thing happening, when it did happen, I turned into Norman Wisdom! With a very high-pitched voice, I started to call for my boss, who was working upstairs.

The second time this happened was years later, at a Christian meeting I had been speaking at. After the meeting had finished, food and drinks were provided in another room. Before I knew what was happening, this lady made a pass at me. I must admit, part of me was enjoying it, as it was doing wonders for my ego. However, I knew I had to get out of the situation, so I suggested that we went and joined the others.

As I left the house to drive back home, I passed this lady at the bus stop. It was pouring with rain, and I had two voices speaking to me. One was saying, 'Pull over and give her a lift home.' The other was saying, 'Keep driving. Don't stop.' You will be pleased to hear that I chose to listen to the latter. I drove back to Sheffield, breaking the speed limit. I went straight to my friend's house, got him out of bed and asked him to pray for me.

Paul knew what he was talking about when he said, 'Flee the evil desires of youth' (2 Tim. 2:22). In *The Message* it reads, 'Run away from infantile indulgence.' Three days later I received a letter from this lady asking me if we could meet up. She also informed me that she had been having an affair with her minister. So once again I went to see my friend, and this time showed him the letter. He prayed for me and we destroyed it.

Unfortunately, like most young men, I mixed up the difference between lust and love. Desperate for love and intimacy, I pursued my lustful desires and became addicted to masturbation and the world of fantasy. As we know, Satan is a slimy beggar. He knows the weak areas in our lives, and that's where he aims his lies and accusations. The Bible says, 'We take captive every thought to make it obedient to Christ' (2 Cor. 10:5).

A few years ago a film came out entitled *American Pie*. This was a comedy about four young men and their ambition to lose their virginity at their graduation party. There is one clip in it where the mother of one of the guys makes a pass at one of the other three. As soon as I saw this part of the film, it triggered all my emotions and thoughts of the past and my fantasy with older women. I knew I would have to make an agreement with my wife, my friends and myself not to watch that film again. Ephesians says, 'And do not give the devil a foothold' (Eph. 4:27). This is what I am trying to do now. I cannot say I always succeed, but I am getting better.

So in conclusion, I want to ask you to be honest with yourself, God and your friends when you work through the questions.

Questions

- What fantasies are you still struggling with?
- Can you masturbate without fantasizing?
- Should we 'scratch the itch'?
- Is it OK for a married man to masturbate?
- Do you stay up late watching films that you know are not helpful for you to be watching?
- Are you taking captive your thoughts, or are they taking you captive?
- Do you need to make yourself accountable to someone concerning the things you read, watch, log onto on your computer or fantasize about?
- If Jesus was tempted in every way, as we are, yet was without sin (Heb. 4:15), was he ever tempted by sex? What do you think?
- Is your life ruled by love or lust?
- Do you have control over your fantasies or do they have control over you?

The test of real character is what a man does when he is tired.

Attributed to Winston Churchill

5

Kingdom vs. Church?

Lee

This was probably the most challenging chapter from Dead Men
Walking, *especially for church leaders. (Maybe this was the chapter
that a senior church figure in the UK complained to our publishers
about!) Many of them have helped me think it through even more,
while others may have decided to ignore it.*

*I have realized that it's vital that we Christians should try to
get on with those whom we don't totally agree with (we could
even invite them to speak in our churches!). It keeps us sharp and
the debates remain fresh. I know of many churches who just dip
into the same pool of speakers for years and years, and if those
speakers aren't keeping themselves fresh, that will adversely affect
those churches' effectiveness and growth.*

*We learn by being exposed to stuff that challenges us. That's
why I go to the cinema! The journey I have been on here in Leeds
makes this chapter very pragmatic for me, especially as we have
lacked big churches that can make the city's Christian heart rate
look healthy.*

---

*He will always give you all you need from day to day if you will
make the Kingdom of God your primary concern.*
Luke 12:31, TLB

If you're looking for a deep theological discussion about
the kingdom, liberation theology, deconstructionist theology,
dominion theology, dispensationalist theology, and other long

words I could make up, then I'm afraid you're not going to find them in this chapter! In fact this is not the book to be reading – get a proper one! I have done some theological training, but I am by no means an academic theologian – as most, if not all, of my friends will tell you. In this chapter I'm going to just share some ideas on how a kingdom mindset slotted into place for me, without me even knowing it.

I am not mad after all!

I started on a course called 'Equipped to Lead' in September 1997. I went to a residential weekend in Derbyshire with hundreds of other delegates starting a whole year of study in theology and practical leadership training. For the first three or four sessions God spoke to me so much, it was almost unbelievable. What he said was, quite simply, that I wasn't mad after all. We were getting teaching on several issues around the kingdom of God and also Christocentric theology (i.e. Jesus being the centre of everything we do). I hadn't known what I really thought about the kingdom of God, but I just realized that as an evangelist type, I saw myself as a kingdom-builder, not necessarily a church-builder. This is quite strange because I am in real life a loyal member of a church. However, being kingdom-focused does not mean that you don't believe in local church, as one church leader I had met thought. It just means that you believe in kingdom growth and not necessarily church growth (I hope this will stimulate some discussion!). As a friend of mine said, he'd read all the church growth books and he just didn't get it or want it! So as I sat being taught about the kingdom of God and different interpretations of it, it was fascinating to me that I had already come to these conclusions without ever having been taught the theology behind them. And the 'Equipped to Lead' course was, for me, just like putting some cement in the foundations that I had already started to build.

*The church is but the result of the coming of God's kingdom
into the world by the mission of Jesus Christ.*
Attributed to H.D. Wendland

The kingdom is fascinating, as the present is bound up with
the future. We live between the already and the not-yet. We
already have the down payment, the guarantee, but there
is still more to come. One of the pastors featured in the
Transformations video said, 'I realized that I wouldn't be held
accountable for how I led my church, but for how I pastored
my city.' The church leader who can think along those lines
is very powerful indeed – one who looks to build their city,
and the kingdom of God in their city and beyond.

Even though I want to stay in Leeds to see God move, I also
feel the need to go and serve other places. For instance, I was
involved in 'Message 2000' in Manchester, because I wanted
to go and serve Manchester. If you know anything about the
North of England, you'll know that traditionally we in Leeds
sing rude songs about Manchester! The paradox is that as you
dig deeper and seek to build the kingdom where you are, you
actually get a wider view to break denominational barriers
and other boundaries, and serve people elsewhere.

We are not just Jesus to our church, we are Jesus to our
city – and that influences everything we do. I've done a lot
of evangelistic activities and, if I am honest, they have mostly
been about putting 'bums on seats' on Sunday morning. We
must challenge ourselves to think, 'Can we do evangelism to
build someone else's church, or even put people into a church
experience which is far outside of our own?' That is where
the rubber hits the road.

God still astounds me with the things he does. Many people
just try to build their own little (or big) church, but God,
being God, says, 'You go to build the kingdom, and build the
city that you live in, and I will build my church in the process!'
That's the amazing grace that he has. If the church is the body,

as it says in 1 Corinthians 12, then the body must be used. We're told to go and bear fruit. And how does a body go and bear fruit? It needs to go and do things! Simple, isn't it? Why do people make Christianity so complicated?

The church is the community of the kingdom
but never the kingdom itself.
Anonymous

The body of Jesus Christ needs to be active. We hear a lot about the church being the body of Christ, and different parts of it. I've even done assemblies in primary school about being the little finger of the body. But actually it's about putting the body into action. 'And Christ gave gifts to people – he made some to be apostles, some to be prophets, some to go and tell the Good News, and some to have the work of caring for and teaching God's people. Christ gave those gifts to prepare God's holy people for the work of serving, to make the body of Christ stronger' (Eph. 4:11, 12 NCV).

It's really interesting that Paul talks about the 'five-fold ministry' as preparing God's people for the work of service, not just preparing God's people to be who they are. The church is not an end in itself but a springboard – a trampoline to serve God's kingdom. Any oppressive church leadership which says otherwise is holding back the kingdom of God.

Fragile

I've spent many hours in meetings with church leaders and it took me a while to realize how fragile some of their jobs are. Sometimes they are simply moving on; or sometimes they've been asked to leave where there's been a struggle that we didn't know was happening in the church; or it may be a moral issue. I'm not saying that this is true for everyone, but maybe some churches are not as radical as they could be because the leaders fear for their jobs all the time, whether that's a paid job or the status involved in eldership or leadership. The most exciting, honest and open church leaders that I've met are the ones who have stuck their necks out for the sake of the kingdom. In Leeds we have been involved in significant dialogues about working together, not in uniformity but in unity in some way, and it's so exciting to see how churches are willing to lay down some of their ideals for the sake of the kingdom. But you can also see people become very concerned for fear of losing their jobs and for fear of losing their whole theology and everything they've been taught over the last ten or twenty years.

He said, 'Go out'; not 'Open the door and ask people to come in quietly, after they have wiped their feet.'

Jesus didn't arrive here on earth, change us, and leave us to the work of having nice Sunday meetings. He left us with the Great Commission – that is, to go out and tell people, and as St Francis of Assisi may have said, 'Use words if you have to.' Jesus didn't say, 'Have open services', or 'Have services that are a bit more lively', and he certainly didn't say, 'Discuss for seventeen hours whether you should start at 6.00 p.m. or 6.30 p.m.'! He said, 'Go out'; not 'Open the door and ask people to come in quietly, after they have wiped their feet.' That's a big difference, and a fundamental issue for a lot of churches in the West. A church that thinks that it's sorted always makes me nervous, and I often prefer the maverick style where people make mistakes but are actually trying to make a difference. Sure, it might not be a slick thing on a Sunday, or whatever day of the week, but it sorts out the men from the boys, or the women from the girls. I've been really blessed, in my previous work in Leeds, to have been financially supported by several of the churches. There are two particular churches I can think of who have given sacrificially to me, and that really blesses me because the people I met weren't necessarily going to end up in their churches. They just saw that I was doing something in the city and they wanted to invest in that. It means they gave money without expecting a return on it. Do we sometimes give, but hope that our giving will benefit us in some way? In Ephesians 4 Paul says that the body of Christ will be made stronger, but that comes after the works of service; so it's as we go out and serve that the church is built, which is the opposite way round to how we've often done it!

Working together

We have a great organization in Leeds called Kidz Klub for unchurched 5–11s. The children are visited every week and taken by bus on a Saturday morning to Bridge Street Church in Leeds. Many churches have taken on a Kidz Klub and have done it excellently (like Frontline Church in Liverpool), but Leeds started it with several churches, all paying for their own buses, and sending their own volunteers to be part of it. It's not owned by anybody, and it's simply building the kingdom of God in Leeds. Who knows what the future will bring from investment in these young people who, without that regular visit and bus ride, would never have heard the name of Jesus? I get quite excited when I hear about 'mega-churches' and the impact they are having, but I'm also stimulated by partnership and low-key networks that are seeking ways to serve the kingdom of God together.

The thing about kingdom values is that they affect you every single day. When making decisions about how to run projects, I've tried to base them on kingdom values. A small charity often has to compete for funds from churches or from trusts, and I decided to be open about where I got my money and how I applied for it, so as not to foster the kind of secret fundraising attitude that a lot of small charities had. The other thing that I'm really keen on is sharing ideas. Nothing's original anyway, and if we're into building the kingdom, then I'm happy to help someone in this country or other countries by passing on the things that God has taught us. 'There's no copyright in the kingdom' is a favourite youth worker's line!

It's so easy to become entrenched in 'church committees', and not actually see the big picture. We're residents of a 'global village', and so we want to see the kingdom of God advance in the world. I want to see the kingdom of God advance in the West, in Europe, in the UK, in England, in Yorkshire, and in Leeds. In the big scheme of things, what I do isn't really that important. I don't want to be driven by a fundamental attitude of 'I want to build everything that's close to me', but rather, I seek to have a kingdom value of 'Let's build this together'. That attitude should be natural to us, but often it isn't. But when you start to see things coming together, it really is very exciting, and I love it when I hear about other people's successes, because that's what it's about. God has given to me, people have given to me, and I want to give back – it's as simple as that. If we are generous, God will be generous to us.

The church is not here to help us study the Bible once a week, but for the release of the kingdom.
Anonymous

Questions (on a postcard!)

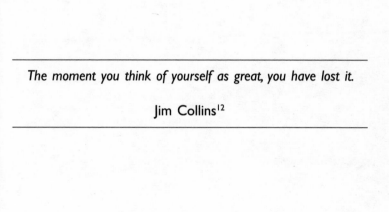

The moment you think of yourself as great, you have lost it.

Jim Collins[12]

6

Free Hugs

Baz

It is amazing that a young man offering free hugs in a shopping mall in Sydney could cause a major reaction, but that is exactly what has happened with Juan Mann. Over 6 million people have been on YouTube to view the moving video of what happened, leaving over 15,000 comments.

Juan Mann wrote a sign saying 'Free Hugs' and began walking up and down Pitt Street Mall, receiving various looks and comments. Eventually, after fifteen minutes, an old lady tapped Juan on the shoulder and asked for a hug. She was feeling upset, as her dog had died that day and it was also the first anniversary of her daughter's death. Juan knelt down and hugged the old lady. She left with a smile on her face. Gradually other people, young and old, began to ask for hugs, and something began which has since snowballed. All around the globe people are offering free hugs.

In Sydney the authorities banned Juan from hugging people and told him he could continue only if he got liability insurance for $25 million in case someone got hurt! Juan did not have this kind of money, so he began a petition and collected 10,000 names saying that they wanted the chance to have a free hug whenever, wherever and from whomever. The authorities backed down and Juan continues to give free hugs to whoever asks for one.[13]

This story and the video really gripped me. When I saw the video, over a year ago, I broke down crying, as I thought it was so moving and so much like what happened to Jesus when he walked this earth. He spent so much time with the ordinary person, eating, drinking and laughing, that the people in authority began to get angry and challenged him about his behaviour. His reply was, 'I have come for these people, not the ones who don't think they are sick and don't need help.'

The *good news* about Jesus is that he came to this earth to hug it. To show each of us how much God loves us and how he wants to help us daily with our struggles, hurts, disappointments and questions. Do not be put off from receiving God's love by what others may think of you.

Recently I have been telling the story of Juan and showing the 'free hugs' film in junior and senior schools, with amazing effects. Teachers have been crying at the end of assemblies, asking me for a hug, and some of the young people have gone home and hugged family members, with unbelievable responses from their parents and brothers or sisters. In one senior school 16-year-old boys were queuing up to receive a hug from me at the end of the assembly. This was such an amazing experience for me and also challenging to the staff and the rest of the pupils, who witnessed as I embraced each young man with a good firm hug, encouraging them to keep reaching out for more love and giving it to others.

Virginia Satir, a family therapist, says we need four hugs per day for survival, eight for maintenance and twelve for growth – so isn't it about time we allowed ourselves to be hugged by a God who loves us? We also need to put ourselves in the place where we can be hugged by our family and friends and not worry about what others think or say.

Let's not say this is not a man thing. Masculinity is being prepared to admit that we need physical affection from other men and not being too macho to acknowledge it.

Whether it's inside or outside the church, all men long to be loved. What better way to show it than to embrace each other in a manly way and not a twee 'Christian Hug'. I want to be hugged and so do the men in the church I am part of. Let's get over the embarrassment factor and excuses that men will be put off God if we hug them. What a load of crap!

Let's be real with ourselves, others and God.

He who does not live in some degree for others,
hardly lives for himself.

Michel de Montaigne (1533–92)

7

And Whatever Did Happen to the Heroes?

Baz

The ordinary man is involved in action, the hero acts.
An immense difference.
Henry Miller[14]

In one of their biggest hits, the Stranglers lamented the lack of heroes in today's world. There is a cry from society today for heroes who will not let down their followers or supporters.

There has never been a more important time than today for young boys, teenagers and men to have heroes – heroes who are going to be good role models and not cause disappointment and disillusionment by their behaviour. The heroes of the political and religious arenas have not escaped media coverage of their misdemeanours in the past, and rightly so.

My first hero

It was while at junior school that I first experienced putting someone in the category of a hero. The person involved was a schoolteacher named Mr Hardy. He was everything I did not have in a father. First, he was there every day. Not like mine, who left to live in Africa. Second, he was funny and was very encouraging to me. He had the ability to make you feel good about yourself even when you were struggling with some aspect of work. He was our football coach, and not only knew about coaching but could play as well. He was a great teacher and could make the most boring subject sound interesting.

The one thing he really got me excited about was the stories and characters in the Bible: Moses, David, Joseph, Elijah, Jesus . . . It was no wonder I won the school Scripture prize that year. What was so amazing was that I became a charismatic Christian before I became a Christian.

Let me explain: every time we had an assembly and sang a hymn or a song, I would start to jump up and down with excitement while singing. The hymn that caused the biggest stir in me was 'O Jesus I have promised'. The staff and other pupils used to look on with puzzlement and amusement. I don't know why Jesus had become a hero to me, especially when I did not know him at that time. Mr Hardy had a great way of making the Bible and its characters come alive.

Why was this teacher a hero of mine? It was because he had the ability to bring out the best in people. He listened to them, encouraged them and believed in them. Even when he disciplined you, you believed it was for your benefit.

Gordon

Senior school was a great time for me. I was into football in a big way, as well as other sports. If I could have done PE all day, I would have been in my element. I did have sporting heroes, but I knew I would never meet them or emulate their achievements.

At school there was a pupil I looked up to. He was a fifth former when I started at the school, and his name was Gordon. I had met Gordon during the summer holidays when a few of us went to play football with some of the staff and pupils from the senior school. He was supposed to be one of the hardest boys in the school.

There was a rumour that some of the staff wanted him to be Head Boy, due to the respect he had from the other pupils (which was not down to his ability to use his fists but down to his character). However, the Head and Deputy Head put a halt to that, since he could not be the kind of Head Boy that people expected. Where do we see that happen time and again? I'll give you a clue – six letters, the first two being 'CH' and the last two being 'CH'. What's missing? 'UR'! Gordon was an all-round sportsman who always gave 100 per cent in everything he did.

When I was 13, I was asked to sign for the under-18s football club, Whessoe Juniors, who played in the Darlington and District Youth League. Gordon was the captain. The manager asked me to bring my boots along for the last game of the season, a cup final. I was to be one of the substitutes, but did not expect to get a game. With about fifteen minutes to go to the end of the game, the manager shouted to me to get warmed up. The next thing I knew, I was on the same field as one of my heroes.

I had been on the pitch about one minute when I got my first touch of the ball. I also got a good clobbering from one of the opponents, and the next thing I knew, I was lying on the grass in agony.

I was not sure if the pain I could feel was coming from my legs or my back or both. I have never been hit by a bulldozer, but I'm sure this came close to what it might feel like. To be honest, I didn't want to get up – it would have been easier to get carried off.

The next thing I heard was Gordon saying, 'Don't worry, I'll get him back. But now get up and don't let the bastard see you are hurt – show him what you can do.' Slowly, but with determination, I got up and started to jog to run off the pain.

Sure enough, true to his word, Gordon returned the compliment to the guy who had fouled me. He did it in such a way that no foul was given but the guy needed to be carried off the pitch and substituted. A quick wink and smile from Gordon to me said it all; he had looked out for me. Although I can't agree now with what he did, boys and men are looking for heroes who will protect, encourage and support them in all they do.

One staff member at senior school made an immediate impression on me – my house master, Miles Burnidge. I never admitted this to my mates, but I admired him for the way he led the house, taught and encouraged people. I remember that in one assembly in my first year, after our house had won the school athletics day, Mr Burnidge was making a speech about how proud he was of everybody who took part, including those who supported the athletes. He went on to say that one pupil had made a major contribution to the team, not just by winning his own four events but by the way he had supported, encouraged and motivated others in the team during the sports day and before, in the training days. I, like many others, assumed he was talking about Gordon. Imagine the feeling of amazement when he called out my name to come and collect the award of the house athletics colours – the first time ever a first year had been given this award in the school. I could not have felt better!

Mr Burnidge was very good at motivating the pupils. He seemed to know just what each pupil needed to feel special and appreciated. He had certainly done this for me during that assembly. He was very soon to become another of my heroes.

Every adult has a responsibility to be a role model or hero
to at least one child.
Brenda Sanson[15]

I wonder if Mr Hardy and Mr Burnidge would agree with this statement. Whether or not they would, they were certainly good role models to me, and I'm almost sure I was not the only one who felt that way.

Brenda Sanson goes on to say: 'Our children need to know that the people we see as heroes do not need to score the winning basket or goal. Our heroes are the people we meet every day of our lives. These are the people who have courage and give unselfishly to others.' This is definitely what I experienced at school. These men were not famous but just ordinary men who obviously loved teaching, showing this by the way they related to the pupils, and in their ability to help others, no matter what background the pupils had come from.

I once heard Gerald Coates say, 'Honour those who have made an impact on your lives and have enhanced them.' These two teachers had done that in my life, so I decided to honour them by inviting them and their wives to my wedding. During my speech at the reception, in front of 200 other guests, I thanked them for being real heroes and for the positive impact they had made in my life during my early years and as a teenager. I hope that one day someone could say the same of me.

Jesus my Hero

It is very interesting as you get older and look back on your life, to see which people have been heroes and role models to you. When I became a Christian at the age of 17, Jesus became one of my heroes and later the Hero. As I discovered more about Jesus, I knew that he is what a real hero is about: sacrificial loving and giving without demanding anything in return for himself.

About seven years ago someone came up to me and said, 'Baz, I just want you to know you are one of my heroes.' I had often wondered what it must be like to be famous and be someone's hero. Well, I'm not famous and never will be, but to be told you are someone's hero is quite frightening. I wondered why he had said this. What were the qualities in my life that caused him to see me as a hero? Did I deserve such a position? Instead of feeling excited or even big-headed, I started to feel fear, curiosity and unrest. I felt afraid of letting him down in the future. What should I do? What would you do? This was so unexpected and had come from such an unlikely source. Having heroes is one thing, but being a hero is quite another.

Two other men also became my heroes when I was younger. One was my Boys' Brigade officer and the other was my youth leader. The Brigade officer, John Lawrence, was a real gentleman and had great patience; he was a very devout and holy man of God. Between the ages of 11 and 15 I attended the 1st Darlington Battalion of the Boys' Brigade and had a great time with lots of friends. Unfortunately peer pressure affected teenagers in the 1970s just like it does today. Some bright spark at the BB Headquarters in London had this wonderful idea of changing the uniform. The old uniform consisted of school trousers, shirt and blazer, with black tie and shoes, and a white sash, belt and cap, which you got from the BB. It was amazing how much pride we took in wearing this and how much effort was put into cleaning it for inspection each week.

So when our captain informed us that the uniform was to change and showed us what the new one looked like, I don't think he or the other officers expected such a reaction. There was nearly a riot! The problem was that the new uniform was a blue shirt with a white tassel on one of the shoulders. It was too feminine for the likes of us 15-year-old Northerners.

It was OK for those Southerners, but not for us!

One lad commented, 'If we have to wear that, we'll all leave!' and this was echoed by a large 'Yeah!' The officers were quite shocked by the response but tried to talk us round to just trying these uniforms. However, true to our words and true to the effect of peer pressure, we all left within two weeks. It must have been hard for the officers, especially after giving so much of their time to us over the years, to see about fifteen young boys leave over something as petty as a new uniform. I had been involved for four years and others a lot longer. But boys will be boys.

Seven years later, while home from college for Christmas, I once again bumped into John Lawrence. I went with my friends to a local Anglican church on Christmas Eve. This was the church I had to go to once a month for Brigade Sunday. This time I was there out of choice, because the Methodist church I was part of did not have a service on Christmas Eve.

I cannot recall anything about the service. At the end of it I was greeted with a huge smile and handshake from John. He looked genuinely pleased to see me and enquired about what I was doing now. When I informed him I had become a Christian and was attending Bible college, he could not stop smiling and told me that every week since the day we left the BB, he had prayed for my friends and I to become Christians. This was when John became a hero in my life. What a man of God! What a saint! What a hero! He had prayed for me faithfully for seven years before he discovered I had become a Christian. He told me that evening that he would continue to pray for me, now that I was living for God.

Every member has to learn the object of the Boys' Brigade and recite it to the captain. When you can do this, you receive a badge to wear on your blazer lapel. The object of the BB is: 'The advancement of Christ's kingdom among boys and the promotion of habits, obedience, reverence, discipline, self-

respect and all that tends towards a true Christian manliness.'
It took me three weeks and probably four attempts before
I could recite it fully to the captain and receive my badge. I
thought I would never be able to do it. It took seven years of
faithful prayer for me before John discovered that his prayers
had been answered. The object was for me to experience for
myself God and his outrageous grace. That is why John was
a hero to me.

Another man to deserve such an accolade was my former
youth leader, Bill Brown. When we used to meet at his
house for youth group every week, I would watch Bill closely,
especially when we were worshipping. Every time we began
to sing songs or hymns to God, Bill would get off his chair
and kneel on the floor, and tears would begin to flow down
his cheeks as he sang and prayed. At first I found this rather
weird and a bit scary, but later I realized that Bill knew how
much God loved him and what Jesus had done for him. Every
time we sang 'Blessed Assurance' we knew Bill would end up
crying. Interestingly, when I sang 'O Jesus I Have Promised' at
my wedding, a similar thing happened to me as I realized the
immensity of God's love and how he had rescued me from
a road of destruction. We need to see more men crying in
times of worship, prayer and fellowship with others, as they
allow their emotions to be touched by the Spirit of God.

Bill was in his late fifties when I first met him and his wife
Ann. They were a great, godly couple, whose house was open
any time of the day. When I look back at Bill's life, I see a
man who was passionate about God and his word and sharing
that word with others. Bill was a Methodist local preacher.
He was very radical in the ways he chose to communicate to
people about Jesus. He would often take young people with
him from the youth group to help him with the service. He
once took two friends of mine with him to a church he was
speaking at. Both Shirley and Ken were gifted people. Shirley
had an amazing singing voice and Ken was an excellent artist.

So while Bill preached, Ken would paint what Bill was talking about, and when he had finished his sermon, Shirley would get up and sing a song in her beautiful soul voice. This was in the late 1970s, before anyone had heard a talk about cultural relevance at Spring Harvest or the like.

One time Ann and Bill had arranged for the youth group to go round for a meal at their house. As the group waited for the food to be brought into the room, Bill brought in a huge turkey dish and placed it on the table, with strict instructions for us not to touch the dish or lift the lid until the rest of the food had been brought in. After about two to three minutes one of the group members decided to look under the turkey dish. Bill and Ann were waiting patiently outside the room, knowing that curiosity would get the better of someone.

The lid was lifted and the contents were revealed – a dishful of feathers, which immediately began to escape from the dish! The more frantic this young man became in his attempt to get them back into the dish, the more they spread all over the room. As the whole group began desperately trying to hide the evidence of what he had done, Bill and Ann walked into the room, to the horror of the group. Expecting a lecture on doing what you are told, the young people were amazed at Bill and Ann's response. Bill got his Bible, read a few verses and then went on to talk about temptation and the consequences of sin. That certainly got their attention!

Bill was my youth leader for just a few years – he died suddenly one Good Friday at the age of 61. A great day for Bill to go and be with the Lord, but a very sad day for Ann, Fraser, their son, and their family, as well as the many people who had the privilege of knowing this loving and godly man.

We probably all have Christian heroes of faith like Booth, Finney, Wesley, Spurgeon, Taylor, Livingstone, Edwards, Moody, Seymour, Luther-King, Lake, Wimber, Watson and Wigglesworth. But after reading the stories of these men, you may have been reminded of others who have been influential in your life and deserve to be called heroes. Here is a list of some of the men still alive today who are my heroes. Some you will have heard of and others you won't, but they have all made a mark on my life: Dave France, Paul Wakelam, Steve Halliwell, John Archer, Steve Lowton, Tim Sokell, Ken Anderson, Roger Ellis, Gerald Coates, Jeff Lucas, Robert Mason, Roger Forster, Peter Nodding, Steve Chalke, Gary Gibbs, John Scotland, Phil Wall and Pete Greig.

All these men, plus others, have made an impact on my life, by the love they have shown me, or by the encouraging words they have spoken to me, or by their words in books or talks which have challenged and provoked me to become more like Jesus. I value too the time and friendship they have given me, to varying degrees. They are heroes for the way they serve and love the greatest hero ever to have walked this earth – Jesus.

Questions

- Who were your childhood heroes? Why?
- Who are your biblical heroes?
- Who are your modern-day heroes of faith?
- What qualities do you see in them that you admire?
- Do you think it's right to have heroes, as a Christian?
- How would you cope if someone informed you that you were their hero?

What's man's first duty? The answer's brief: to be himself.

Henrik Ibsen (1828–1906)

8

Never Been Trained!

Lee

The follow-up to this chapter is in our other book, Cut to the Chase, *as my kids have grown up. Funny how that happens, eh? It's amazing how little time is spent teaching blokes to be better dads and husbands, and that's probably the most important job we do. Here are some honest reflections on being a dad of twins (err, not on becoming a dad of twins!).*

It's Father's Day as I'm writing this chapter, and I've sneaked up to my office to get some thoughts down while Lauren is asleep. That's the great thing about having twins – they're not usually both asleep at the same time, so you're always on the go. Some people have called it 'double trouble', or 'trial by fire'! Rhea and Lauren are our first and last children! We have no real history of twins in our families, so it came as quite a shock. Rhea and Lauren are identical twin girls, born in 1999, and they're great. But sometimes they are just plain hard work; often it is more difficult for me than Clare, as men seem to handle kids very differently to the way women do.

Most men are just not designed to look after children for more than 20 minutes at a time. By about 25 minutes, the man's usually lost interest, he's watching television, and the children are in the kitchen microwaving car batteries!
Jack Dee[16]

Being a dad is an experience I never could have prepared for. Here are a few thoughts, not deep theological theories, about being a dad.

Andy Hickford said, 'I'm the best father in the world . . . when I'm away from home.' I and many of my friends can completely sympathize with that. I often find it very hard being at home with Rhea and Lauren, because it's especially difficult when you've got things to do. But the amazing thing is that I miss them loads as soon as I get to work, or as soon as I go away. That in itself has made me think about my attitude when I'm at home. It's so easy to forget the wonderful gift that children are to us.

Twins!

I went with Clare to the hospital when she went for her first ultrasound scan. We waited with all the other parents, surrounded by 'breast is best' posters. It was the first thing on a Monday morning, and we were the first scan of the week.

The radiologist was warming up the machine; she put the ultrasound sensor on Clare's stomach with that nasty greasy stuff, and immediately she said, 'I've got something to tell you – you're having twins!'

Clare and I just looked at each other, completely aghast, and Clare gently started to cry (I think tears of joy!).

It was amazing as the nurse gradually described how they were lying and how they were intertwined with each other, and whose leg was whose and which arm was which! Those ultrasound pictures still look like ink blots to me, but being there and seeing them in motion, I could actually work out limbs, heads and even hearts.

People never say on their deathbed, 'I wish I'd spent more time at work.'
Anonymous

So things were fairly straightforward as far as the pregnancy was concerned, apart from Clare being very big. It got to the point, towards the end, where she could have pushed a wheelbarrow in front of her just to take the load off for a while! With seven weeks to go, we started to clear out the spare room for the babies. We moved out my DJ equipment (boo!), but we hadn't really bought anything for them yet.

We went to bed as normal, with Clare stacking herself up with pillows and trying to get herself comfortable. Then between 5 and 6 a.m. I heard these very quiet words: 'Lee, I think my waters have broken.' I suddenly burst into action, getting up, getting ready, getting towels, doing all the things I thought I had to do, and if any of you have ever met me, you'll know that I'm not usually awake before midday! So this was quite an achievement, and all of a sudden there we were – babies on the way, nothing bought, and a risk of the babies being dangerously small as they were very premature. It was such a strange feeling, suddenly realizing that I was going to be a dad, and I think I must have gone into autopilot, just going through the motions.

Clare went into labour (while being pumped with steroids), but there was no room at the inn. The special-care baby units in Leeds were full, so we waited for a couple of hours while they rang round different hospitals, and in the end we had to go to Manchester. Clare went in an ambulance with the blue lights flashing, and I was told to follow behind – slowly – without jumping any red lights. I was gutted!

It was a normal delivery and they just needed a little bit of help at the end to come out. Rhea was the first. She was wrapped up tightly because she was so small and all we could see were these two little eyes looking at us. It was amazing to think, 'I've created a human being!' She was then whisked away to be cared for, and then seven minutes later Lauren came out, which is quite typical – she likes to sleep a bit more than Rhea does. We had a quick look at her before she too was whisked away. We didn't see them for a few hours after that, until they were stabilized and assessed.

Nothing could have prepared me for the next six weeks of going into the special care unit, machines bleeping all around us, and occasionally alarms going off, followed by mad rushes of doctors with babies in their arms. It was a very harsh introduction to being a dad – especially as I had to live on hospital food! We prayed a lot for them in the first few weeks. They were always rigged up to alarms which would often go off for various reasons, and that kept us on edge all the time.

While Clare was in hospital with Rhea and Lauren, I had to run around buying things like cots, buggies, blankets and whatever else we needed, as we just hadn't had the opportunity to buy anything at all. My life had changed for ever. Becoming a parent is the one thing that really changes your life, and something that you're not usually trained for. Now Rhea and Lauren are doing well. They are well-developed, normal kids and they are a joy to be with (most of the time!).

I often have to remind myself of the early days when we didn't know whether Rhea and Lauren would live or die, or whether they would have severe disabilities – always a risk for premature babies. And now when they're climbing all over the furniture and digging into my record bag, and calling 999 on my mobile, it's difficult to think back and remember what a gift they are!

Perhaps that's a problem. We don't think back, we don't remember how amazing it was in those first few days – that new feeling of being a dad, friends bringing you cigars and taking you out to wet the baby's head . . . that can all get lost in day-to-day concerns, early mornings, late nights and the pooey nappies.

Baby poo is one part Velcro and one part nuclear waste.
Robin Williams[17]

Fatherhood

Fatherhood isn't talked about much. Do we pretend we are good fathers when really we feel it's a hard slog sometimes? Hearing some honesty from people about how difficult they find it has been helpful for me. Many researchers say that women are able to be 'multi-tasking'. They can do more than one thing at once, and do them all pretty well. But most men have less of that ability, so we must concentrate on one thing at a time. When we're looking after children, that's what we must do. And that's difficult when we've got other things on our mind, or we're distracted. I'm amazed at the multi-tasking of my Mam, who has looked after the girls when I'm at work, and has also managed to shampoo the carpet, clean the oven, and decorate one of the rooms in the house! How she does it, I'll never know. Keeping children entertained is one of the hardest things I've ever had to do, especially combined with the false Christian guilt that you're not meant to be entertaining them, you're meant to be educating them in a godly way.

There can be so much pressure on Christian parents that it's quite hard sometimes just to enjoy yourself with your children. Seeing light at the end of the tunnel is the way we've coped with twins. We jokingly say sometimes, that one baby must be a doddle. It certainly is like being dropped in at the deep end, and if it wasn't for the help of our good friends, and especially our family, we may have sunk instead of swum over the last few years.

Becoming a parent tests what you really do believe. There is a danger that people can end up living their lives through their children, or as Bertrand Russell said, 'The fundamental defect of fathers is that they want their children to be a credit to them.' The insecurities you kept hidden as an adult often come out in you as a parent. So how can we men become good fathers?

To become a father is not hard . . . but to be a father is very hard.
Wilhelm Busch (d. 1908)

I look back to the way my Dad dealt with me, and I'm amazed sometimes at the way he gave me so much freedom but still managed to correct me when I needed it. And I hope that I can find that balance of allowing freedom so I don't become over-protective, and also steering and guiding my children gently to make the right decisions and to live the radical life. I remember Jeff Lucas saying his faith was tested when his grown-up daughter went off to Africa to do a mission trip, even though she was doing just exactly what he'd been preaching for the last twenty years. I appreciate honesty like that, and I believe fathers need to get together more often to share some of the struggles and joys of this fatherhood business.

An attitude of gratitude

Trying to maintain the right attitude is often half the battle. Having twins provokes all sorts of reactions in people, but one of the strangest was when I was walking with Rhea and Lauren in the buggy together and someone stopped us. Usually people coo over the girls and ask the same questions again and again, but this person just stopped and shook his head. 'Phew, that must be hard work!' he said and he walked off! I knew a guy who had just had kids, and you would have thought he had got a disease. I never heard a positive word from him, and as his kids were slightly older than mine, he used to be the prophet of doom. 'Wait until they get their injections!' 'Wait until they get their first teeth!'

Yes, it is hard work, but Clare and I have tried to keep the attitude that they are an amazing gift and it is a privilege to bring up two young women of God. In fact it's the most important job that we can ever do – to invest our lives into our children.

Before you become a dad, talk to one! And remember – the world doesn't need father figures; it needs dads.

Questions

- Do you enjoy your kids?
- In the book *Man and Boy*, Tony Parsons suggests that there are new starts when we get it wrong, but the dream is still to get it right first time. Discuss.
- How does your relationship with your dad affect your relationship with your kids?

The devil can cite scripture for his purpose.

William Shakespeare, *The Merchant of Venice*

9

'Me, Change? Impossible' – Or is it?

Baz

'Do you think I can really change?' is a question we ask ourselves, or other people, at some point in our lives.

A couple of years ago this was the question I asked myself and my wife Linda in connection with how angry I was feeling towards God and others because of incidents that had occurred in my life. I decided to go and see a counsellor and try to work through these feelings, hoping this would help me change.

Counselling

So, armed with the four reasons why I was angry towards God and others, I embarked on seeing a counsellor. What was so exciting about meeting Dave fortnightly was that he was not a space cadet, but a man who had experienced life and also had been involved in church leadership and knew the pressures and fears I was feeling. My opinion of male counsellors until I met Dave was that they were all like Frasier or Niles Crane from the *Frasier* show. More screwed up than their clients, with bigger needs themselves. What I did not expect during these times was to be challenged to repent over certain attitudes and to discover what the root issue was. But through this I was able to understand why I would react in certain ways at certain times and was able to let go of the anger and move into a better place.

Most men are unable to set aside the anger long enough to bring the true hurt (the root of their anger) to the surface for healing.
Gordon Dalbey[18]

So can you and I change? The answer is a big 'Yes'. But often we wonder what good it will do to remember all the things of the past that hold us back — all our excess baggage. We may think, *I don't want to change and don't need to* or *Yes, I have problems, but don't we all?* This can lead to being 'secure in our insecurities', which can lead to 'pity me parties', and using our problems to get our own way and manipulate others.

The doors we open and close each day decide the lives we live.
Flora Whittemore[19]

When I was a teenager I would often go to the River Tees in my hometown of Darlington. My friends and I would spend the whole day swimming and fishing. The latter was of no interest to me, as I could not understand how or why anyone would find this exciting. Especially the combination of maggots and fish!

However, two of my friends, Graham and Steve, were fanatical about fishing and would try to get me to see the reason why, but to no avail. I would walk up the river about 200 yards and begin throwing half-bricks into the water, thinking this would help them in their endeavour of catching fish. I thought that the fish would swim away from the bricks right into and onto the hooks of my mates. This did not work but I did get a load of abuse from some angry anglers who told me to go away in Russian or Czechoslovakian, I think. All I could remember was the last word — 'Off!'

I remember one day Graham showing all of us how to cast out the fishing line. He was doing really well when all of a sudden he said, 'That's funny — the line is stuck.'

Hooks

Unbeknown to Graham, just as he had been casting out, a friend of my brother, called John, had run behind him, and the hook had got caught in his calf. As Graham kept tugging at his fishing rod, the hook went deeper into John's calf. When he realized what had happened, Graham put his rod down and went to help the screaming John. Blood was pouring out of John's leg as Graham cut the line to disconnect him from the rod.

I asked Graham what we should do. He replied, 'We need to take the hook out.'

But John said, 'No, I'm fine, honest! I'll be OK.'

And he got up off the ground and hobbled away. We quickly caught him and pinned him down whilst Graham removed the hook.

Now, anyone who does fishing will know that a tool called a discourger is used to do this. It is slid down the line and gently removes the hook from the fish's mouth, supposedly without causing any pain or damage. The fish is then thrown back into the river or placed in a net at the riverbank. However, on a human's leg it is a different kettle of fish! (Sorry, I couldn't resist that.) Graham tried to do the same on John's leg that he had done hundreds of times on a fish. Obviously, John was apprehensive, and the rest of us just watched silently. With little difficulty and some pain, the hook was removed. John was now free, and there was only a bit of blood and, no doubt, a small scar in the future to show for the unfortunate accident.

Just like John's initial reaction, we would rather run around doing our normal activities than face some initial pain and have the hooks removed that cause us so much pain and anger. We don't want to face change, because of the discomfort and fear. It is not until you and I admit our fears that we will or can change.

The key to change is to let go of fear.
Roseanne Cash[20]

*Sometimes it's the smallest decisions that can
change your life forever.*
Keri Russell[21]

So, if you are still asking yourself, 'Can I be free from the hurt, pain, anger, shame, abuse, disappointment, fear, resentment or rejection?' – the answer is a big 'Yes', no matter what life has thrown at you, no matter what lie you have been living.

Change is possible firstly, by admitting that you need help and that Jesus can give you that help. By getting to know God intimately, you will receive healing and freedom from whatever is holding you back. Getting closer to God is about him changing you inwardly, which will affect how you behave outwardly.

We want to change but are afraid. Why are we afraid? We are afraid to let God into an area of our lives, as we have managed to cope with it for all these years, even though it is killing the life of God out of us.

- We're afraid of what others might think when they hear what our problem is.
- We don't want to even acknowledge that we have a problem.
- We're scared of change, as we're not sure what the outcome will be.
- Initially, trying to address the problem could make things worse.

It is far riskier staying where you are than moving on from your present position.

Fullness of life

When we began our Christian life, we began a journey with Jesus, and that continues as the days, weeks, months and years pass by. Jesus loves us too much to allow us to stay the same. He offers fullness of life. This is why we need to let him change us so that we can have this fullness. It is far better letting God remove the hooks in our lives than keeping them. Yes, initially it might hurt. In the long term we may still have the memories, but we'll no longer have the emotional ties of the excess baggage that hinders our lives and stops us being the men God wants us to be.

Don't let the fear of change stop you from being set free from all that hinders. Seek help now. Talk to your best friend and allow someone to journey with you as you begin the first step of moving out of the old into the new. It will take a lot of guts but it will be worth it. Believe me. I am so pleased I sought help, as I now know I am a better man for it and a better husband and friend. I am determined to continue. When God shows me an area in my life that he wants to deal with, I want to allow him permission quickly so that I can discover more of his love in my life. What about you?

Liberty means responsibility. That is why most men dread it.

George Bernard Shaw (1856–1950)

10

Practically Spiritual

Lee

I've been really challenged recently by meeting some crazy Welsh people![22] The amazing people from Emerge Wales came to meet some friends of mine in Leeds. They are about as crazy, charismatic and whacky as you could probably ever imagine. The first time I met them was at a 'welcome curry'. This meant trying to grab a meal while people prayed for each other and got 'drunk' in the Spirit, slurring their words and falling into their curries while shouting 'Shabba!' What a night! They continued for the next few days, praying for people in crazy ways and seeing amazing things happen on the streets of Leeds.[23] It was a real breath of fresh air for me and Clare, especially as I lived through the mad 'Toronto Blessing' years when I started out as a youth worker.

Breath of fresh air, yes, but at the same time I was challenged by what was happening, because I realized that there is an intense practicality to my spirituality, while for these guys there is a great need and expectation for miracles. They love and serve the poor, but they also do crazy things like camping out on roadsides and praying with people in the middle of city centres.

I was really challenged by the danger of writing a book like *Cut to the Chase*. We can concentrate on the practical – 'We need to make good choices, and to live our lives as men of God' – and yet I wonder if we can go too far down that road and almost take God out of the mix. Christianity can so easily become a lifestyle with no reliance on God whatsoever.

We need to learn to be 'practically spiritual' – to be intensely practical and miracle-expecting men at the same time. We need to find a way to get the balance right.

Can we be partners with God, in his battle, with his tools, seeing with his perspective?
Linda Harding[24]

David and Goliath

In 1 Samuel 17, we see the familiar story of David and Goliath – a small boy with a catapult against a WWE wrestler! Goliath was 'The Man', but David was the 'but God' lad. That's the phrase that made the difference here – 'but God'.

David approached Goliath after picking up a few stones, and went *with* God *and* his catapult to face the Terminator.

David took his shepherd's staff, selected five smooth stones from the brook, and put them in the pocket of his shepherd's pack, and with his sling in his hand approached Goliath.

As the Philistine paced back and forth, his shield bearer in front of him, he noticed David. He took one look down on him and sneered – a mere youngster, apple-cheeked and peach-fuzzed.

The Philistine ridiculed David. 'Am I a dog that you come after me with a stick?' And he cursed him by his gods.

'Come on,' said the Philistine. 'I'll make roadkill of you for the buzzards. I'll turn you into a tasty morsel for the field mice.'

David answered, 'You come at me with sword and spear and battle-ax. I come at you in the name of GOD-of-the-Angel-Armies, the GOD of Israel's troops, whom you curse and mock. This very day GOD is handing you over to me. I'm about to kill you, cut off your head, and serve up your body and the bodies of your Philistine buddies to the crows and coyotes. The whole earth will know that there's an extraordinary GOD in Israel. And everyone gathered here will learn that GOD doesn't save by means of sword or spear. The battle belongs to GOD – he's handing you to us on a platter!'

That roused the Philistine, and he started toward David. David took off from the front line, running toward the Philistine. David reached into his pocket for a stone, slung it, and hit the Philistine hard in the forehead, embedding the stone deeply. The Philistine crashed, face-down in the dirt.

That's how David beat the Philistine – with a sling and a stone. He hit him and killed him. No sword for David!

Then David ran up to the Philistine and stood over him, pulled the giant's sword from its sheath, and finished the job by cutting off his head. When the Philistines saw that their great champion was dead, they scattered, running for their lives.

The men of Israel and Judah were up on their feet, shouting! They chased the Philistines all the way to the outskirts of Gath and the gates of Ekron. Wounded Philistines were strewn along the Shaaraim road all the way to Gath and Ekron. After chasing the Philistines, the Israelites came back and looted their camp. David took the Philistine's head and brought it to Jerusalem. But the giant's weapons he placed in his own tent.

I Samuel 17:40–54, *The Message*

David had got it right here: 'I will take the shot, but God is with me.' He was practically spiritual. If another soldier on David's side had done it, it would have been practical, but not spiritual. Manly but not Godly. We need to learn to somehow hold them both in tension.

When I do a presentation, I expect/ask God to help me, but I also spend hours preparing it (and, of course, I am gifted to do it, like David knew how to fire a catapult).

When I am on a see-saw in the playground with my kids, as soon as I get on, they shoot up in the air! It takes both of them on the opposite end to balance me out. It just doesn't work with me on one end and a 10-year-old on the other – it's out of balance.

Over the years I have seen people I know fall off the Christian see-saw by being 'too practical' and self-centred, or by being too spiritual, so that they become untouchable and unaccountable. At either end of this see-saw, feedback is not an option. Without 360-degree feedback, we are all in trouble – every one of us, whether we are 'spiritual' or 'practical'. We need an honest friend to talk to.

What's so great about God is that he wants to do everything with us anyway! I love that. As I sit here on my own (like Norman-no-mates) in a cafe writing this, God wants to use me to teach others about him – scary stuff.

Living by faith

I recently went self-employed instead of full-time employed, and after nine months of 'going it alone', I realized that in lots of ways that was exactly what I had done – gone it alone. I have had to realize, as David did, that it's being partners with God that makes the difference.[25]

I have made a transition from 'self-employed, pushing every door I could', to 'self-employed, realizing that I'm just living by faith really'. That's helped me enormously; it's restored some balance to my life.[26]

I got God onto the see-saw again.

A lot of good lessons here can be learnt from the Hebrew worldview. In Hebrew it's more about 'our God' than 'my God'. It's a whole different way of thinking. There is less about personal salvation. Their way of thinking is more like 'what *our* God is doing'. That worldview is so obvious when you meet a non-Western Christian. It almost screams out of them. We in the West continue to blindly follow the Greek worldview, which is all about 'my God' , 'my salvation', my private 'prayer-time' and 'I think, therefore *I* am'.

The world is the theatre of God's glory.
John Calvin (1509–64)

Being totally self-centred is quite easy to do – just look at the diva-type celebrities. Even the *Big Brother* wannabes can aspire to this very quickly. Once you become totally self-centred, you are really saying 'I am God', and immediately everyone then becomes your servant. That can happen to bosses, pop stars and leaders very easily. Watch a TV documentary about a famous person, and watch this get played out as shops close to help them shop without the common people being there. And just under the surface of this attitude is a hidden misery.

I even saw this intense selfishness the other day at my local post office. I was queuing up to post a parcel and there was a lady there queuing up to buy a lottery scratch-card. But when she got her scratch-card, she suddenly changed. It was like she morphed into someone else, half snatching the card from her friend behind the counter and then almost cowering in a corner to find out whether she had won or not. She bought five tickets while I was there, spending ten quid in five minutes and not winning a thing. Her addiction made her a god-like diva for a few minutes. I wonder how many more she bought that week. She, like many others, had become self-centred, and that in itself can become an addiction, just like scratch-cards.

It's stories of imperfect heroes that keep me going when I need inspiration. My friend Mark Roques[27] told me about George Cadbury recently:

George Cadbury was born in Edgbaston near Birmingham in 1839. His father, John Cadbury, was a tea and coffee dealer. The Cadbury family were members of the Society of Friends and they sent George to the local Quaker School. His childhood was spent in a loving and deeply religious family. At the age of 22 George and his elder brother, Richard, took over the family business and in 1873 they stopped selling tea and coffee and concentrated on chocolate. Their name is now a byword for excellent confectionery that many of us consume on a weekly/daily basis. As Christians, both men believed strongly that the happiness and well-being of their employees was one of the chief aims of the business. They were quite happy to make an honest 'coin' but not at their employees' expense.

Both of the Cadbury boys loved sport. George loved football, cricket, tennis, swimming and golf. George admitted late in life that the first thing he turned to in his daily paper was the cricket news. He was also keen on early morning cold baths!

What was it like to work in the Cadbury chocolate factory? Well, each day began with Bible readings and prayers for all! The working day was considerably shorter than in many other factories of the time. George introduced half-days on Saturdays and bank holiday closing. In 1893, when the premises became too small, George decided to build a factory in the country. They called this new site 'Bournville'. On this site the brothers provided football and cricket fields, a huge playground for children, swings and even an open-air swimming pool! Utterly unheard of at the time.

Employees were encouraged to have fun and the sporting and recreational facilities were fantastic. Sometimes Cadbury would tell his employees to knock off early and everyone would enjoy playing and watching a cracking game of cricket. On one occasion the brothers took all eleven wickets in a match. George once bought his employees a bicycle of the bone-shaker type, which they used to learn to ride during the lunch-break.

Inside the factory there were warm cloakrooms for drying wet clothes and kitchen facilities for cooking food. The brothers also built superb houses for their employees. Every house had a spacious garden for growing vegetables. Fruit trees were planted and the gardens were dug over before each new owner moved in. Trees were planted along the wide roads. Imagine moving from a rat-infested slum dwelling to a wonderful garden estate! You would probably shout – 'The kingdom of God is here!' Later George built schools and a shopping area for his employees. Cadbury campaigned for old-age pensions and fought against grim 'sweated' labour. He even paid £60,000 of his own money into pension funds for his employees.

On his estate he had a special building constructed and each year thousands of deprived children found in the spacious grounds every delight that could appeal to them – swings and cricket, races and games and above all the open-air swimming pool. When George died in 1922, his funeral was attended by over 16,000 people.

What can we learn from the life of George Cadbury? God wants all people to enjoy meaningful work which makes them smile and chuckle. We know from the Bible that God hates oppression, injustice and slavery. God loves to watch grown-ups and children having fun and enjoying his rich creation. That is why he created us in the beginning. The teaching of Jesus is filled with God's commandments. Love God and love your neighbour. George Cadbury responded in an imaginative way to the gospel message. He manufactured first-rate confectionery to the glory of God. His employees could hear and see the biblical message.

Finding the balance

George was great – I only wish more businesses were like his nowadays. George Cadbury was profit-sensitive, but not profit-obsessed. That made a successful, very profitable, people-focused business. He managed to find the balance of being both practical and spiritual.

I was talking to my friend John about my future recently, and he has a reputation for being annoyingly right! He's a trained NLP (Neuro Linguistic Programming) practitioner and messes with your head – in a good way, of course. I talked for about an hour about my hopes, dreams and frustrations. He listened, and listened, and listened, and then very calmly, he said to me, 'I know what you *don't* want to do, Lee. But what do you *want* to do?".

He was right! I was focused so much on the practical stuff that I completely missed the bigger questions such as 'What am I gifted for?' and 'What do I want to do with God?' John helped me to re-focus.

Yes, it's me, but it's also God. God made me (with a little parental help!). Maybe I should have asked him to be more involved in my immediate future, instead of just reacting against the things I didn't want to be.

If we partner with God, we can learn to respond and not just react. That makes us much more fruitful. Being pragmatic, but also expectant of what God will do, helps us to respond appropriately, and not just react or work out of guilt.

And lastly . . .

I was in a *really* boring church service a few weeks ago, and the minister was coldly reading out of his prayer book in a monotone, middle-class voice. As he read, he said, 'Come, Holy Spirit' several times. After the third time I felt like shouting out, 'Watch out – he might, you know!' But I was practical and I kept my mouth shut.

Questions

- Where do you take the reins, when God should take them?
- When did you last talk to God about your job?
- Who is on your see-saw!? Do you need to re-balance?
- Maybe confess times of being over-spiritual too. Where have you talked a good game but your lifestyle didn't match up?
- Who can help you keep this balance?

Eating words has never given me indigestion.

Attributed to Winston Churchill (1874–1965)

11

Crying is for Wimps

Baz

Crying, for men, has always been looked upon as a soft option. Rather than just letting the tears flow, biting your bottom lip and making sure you do not embarrass yourself by doing the 'woman thing' is always a priority.

Many people today still think that a man crying is a sign of weakness and should not happen in public. From an early age most boys are told to stop crying by their parents, family or teachers and act grown up. So crying is frowned upon: it's not what real boys and men do. Crying has had so much bad press lately that I want to persuade you that it is a man thing and a healthy thing for all of us.

Jeremy Clarkson of *Top Gear* fame wrote a couple of newspaper articles in the past slating men for crying, including statements such as 'Men are very confused at the moment.' He suggested that it was not normal for a man to cry and seemed unhappy about men being seen crying in public. Whether it was David Beckham crying as he dropped off his son, Brooklyn, for his first day at school, or other sporting celebrities blubbering away after winning a sporting event, or film stars at an awards ceremony, Clarkson's article was adamant that this ridiculous behaviour must stop.

Why is it that men are embarrassed about other men or, more importantly, themselves crying? The main reason, I suggest, is that we do not want to be seen as weak. Well, here's something to consider:

Crying is not a sign of weakness but a sign of strength. When a man cries, he is being strong, not weak, as he is allowing his real self to come out from behind the mask — the man he was made to be.

Stop crying!

My first vivid memory of crying uncontrollably was when I was 10, after a fight at junior school. I was stood crying in front of a teacher, being told to 'Stop crying *now!*' The harder I tried to stop, the more I cried and the more the teacher kept raising his voice, saying, 'Stop crying!' *I would if I could,* I thought, but I had been hurt physically as well as my pride. That was the beginning of making sure I was never to be seen crying in public, no matter what happened.

At the age of 15 my life was to change forever, but not the way I anticipated. I was given the opportunity to have a two-week football trial with a professional club. A dream come true for any young lad! Things were going really well until the third day. The first-team players and I were lying on the playing field recovering from doing some sprinting — when it happened. The player coach came up to me and grabbed my testicles. He did not say anything and neither did the players who saw this. I was totally confused and angry, so I just told him to get lost. At the end of the training session I just got changed without getting a shower and never went back, pretending to my friends that I failed the trial.

As a result of this incident, the anger continued to build up for the next ten years, and it would manifest itself whenever I played football or rugby. It would be vented on any of my opponents' heads or legs, depending on the game. As I continued carrying this hurt around, I was determined to be a man and not cry over spilt milk. No one was going to hurt me again and I was never going to tell anyone what happened.

When I was 17 I thought I was in love, and when the girl of my dreams ended our relationship whilst we were at a party, I was devastated. So I got drunk, went to the bathroom and began punching the wall and crying. 'Don't worry, there's plenty more fish in the sea,' my mates kept trying to encourage me. I didn't want a fish – I wanted one particular girl. Angry and drunk, I left the party thinking everyone was out to get what they could to make themselves happy, no matter who they hurt – and I was exactly the same.

Deciding that life stinks, I took an overdose of pills with more drink and ended up in hospital having my stomach pumped. Eventually, after three or four days, I discharged myself and tried to get on with life and do the 'man thing' – filling my life with business rather than facing the problems head on. However, the anger now had other ingredients to add to the mix: depression, isolation, misunderstanding and embarrassment all blended together, making one mixed-up man – me.

I used to work as a central heating engineer, and I would often just begin to cry in someone's house whilst working. This was not due to me flooding the place but was because of what was going on internally. I would quickly excuse myself, go to the bathroom and compose myself so my boss would not see me like that. Something deep was going on in my life but I had no understanding of what it was.

Six months later, God ambushed my life in an amazing way as I discovered that Jesus was real, not a myth, and that his life, death and resurrection could and would turn my whole life upside down as I began to follow him. I continued journeying with God in my new life, but was never sure if he was interested in the areas of my life that really hurt. So I did not tell anyone what happened when I was 15.

Well, this behaviour went on until I was 26 and at a conference in Sheffield. I was one of 2,000 people who had come to hear a man called John Wimber speak. During this conference God once again astounded me by what he did.

One of Wimber's team came up to me and said, 'When you were 15 you were sexually interfered with, and God wants to heal you of the pain that this caused.'

I tried not to show any emotion and just said to this guy, 'I'm sorry – you're wrong.'

He humbly apologized and left.

What the hell was that? I thought as I left. *Who has been talking to him?*

The next day this guy came up to me again, saying the same thing and apologizing for any discomfort this was causing me, but urging me to talk to someone I trusted, as this could be the beginning of knowing real freedom and healing.

Taking a risk

That night I decided to take a risk and tell my mate Steve what had happened when I was 15. Thoughts like *What if he rejects me? What if he says he doesn't want to be my friend any more?* were spinning around in my mind. Well, after what seemed an age, I told him and his wife. I sat there waiting for him to reply, 'You dirty git! Get out of my house! I never want to see you again!' in a Geordie accent. As I waited, the silence was deafening. He then just came over to me and hugged me. Something broke and the floodgates opened. I cried like a little lost child, weeping uncontrollably. Tears and snot began to run out onto his shirt but he still hugged me. A huge dam had burst and there was no turning back. This was when this hard Northern lad began to become a soft, gentle man who is not afraid of tears and now cries at pretty much anything and everything.

Put the macho stuff on hold for a while guys. Find the strength within yourself to open up your heart and give yourself permission to cry, cry, cry . . . for whatever reason. You'll always come out a better man because of it.
Hogan Hilling[28]

Men crying

For the first seventeen years of my life I never saw a man cry publicly. The first person I saw who seemed not to be bothered by what others thought of him was my youth leader, Bill Brown.

My mates and I would go around his house for our youth group night, and when we had a time of prayer and worship, that's when it would happen. *The big tear jerk!* I thought. Bill would kneel on his carpet as we prayed and sang. I would always look at him wondering why the tears were falling down his face constantly as we sang 'What a friend we have in Jesus', and thinking *What the hell is up with him?*

Years later, I now understand that Bill was overwhelmed with God's love, forgiveness and healing, and when this happens to me, I am thankful to Bill for role modelling to me that it was OK then and still OK now for a man to cry.

Let your tears come. Let them water your soul.
Eileen Mayhew[29]

Tearful Clarkson says: 'We want our hamster back'[30]

This was the headline. Jeremy Clarkson in tears? Yes, if the Daily Express's reporting was accurate. Could this be the same Jeremy Clarkson who, only two years earlier, in his article in the *Sun* had slammed men for crying? When I read that headline, I was really excited, as it appeared that Clarkson did not allow his mind and his previous thoughts to stop him from expressing what was going on in his heart.

Phil Donahue once said, 'I think people who never cry are like people who never laugh: there is something wrong with them.'[31] This is so true. Most men don't know how to give themselves permission to release the pain, because of those hindering words, 'Big boys don't cry.'

The article went on to say that Clarkson fought back tears as he visited his friend Richard Hammond in hospital. He was fighting for his life after crashing at 280 m.p.h. in a jet-powered car while filming for the TV show *Top Gear*. Clarkson was quoted as saying, 'We want our Hamster back.'

Whenever someone you are close to is on the brink of death, theories go out the window and reality kicks in – just like it did for Jeremy Clarkson.[32]

Real men weep

In the Bible we read that 'Jesus wept' (John 11:35) when he heard about his close friend Lazarus's death. This is the shortest verse in the Bible, and the one with the biggest impact. Try to imagine Jesus, the Son of God, weeping in public like that. He was a real human being, with real human feelings.

We need to realize that crying can and does bring healing from things that have caused us great pain. I often pray for men that God would replace their tears of sadness with tears of joy. As men we mostly find it difficult to express openly the pain we feel and to allow ourselves to be vulnerable.

Crying can make you a better man

Since God began to soften my heart and make it more pliable, I have cried so much and still do, whether it be watching a Kleenex advert, reading Gordon Ramsay's autobiography, crying over a friend's death or just seeing someone being honoured. I am so excited that I have been able to express what I'm feeling through the action of tears.

What soap is for the body, tears are for the soul.
Jewish proverb

In the Bible, we are told there is 'a time to weep and a time to laugh, a time to mourn and a time to dance' (Ecclesiastes 3:4). Why not allow yourself the time for tears and then laughter? By doing so you will begin to break the power of the lie that 'crying is for wimps'.

No man was ever great by imitation.

Samuel Johnson (1709–84)

12

The False Divide

Lee

During my twenty-plus years in the church in the UK, I've noticed with fascination that there are some things in church culture that are taught as if they are in the Bible, when really they are not. There are things that are 'implied' but not even mentioned. One example is the great chasm that is supposed to exist in society between the sacred and the secular.

I was one of the first Christian DJs, and it was a little bit of a novelty for a while. In the early 1990s no one had ever seen a DJ at a Christian gig before, especially in Christian worship events, and I used a lot of material which came out on Christian record labels. Some of it was very good, like Hydro and much of the dance music which came out at the time, dripping with the Holy Spirit – but I soon realized there was actually very little quality Christian dance music. So I used to just play whatever 'secular' music I liked.

People still come up to me and say, 'Where do you get all your Christian dance music from?' I go to a shop (or a website), pick records off the shelf that I like the look of, pray a bit, listen to the music, and then decide whether or not to buy them. There is nothing more to it than that and I don't fast before I buy! I have got a nose for a good or bad tune and the rest is common sense (or maybe a bit of discernment, if you want to spiritualize it!).

> *The only truly secular thing is sin.*
> Roger Ellis & Chris Seaton[33]

The simple truth is, there is really no such thing as 'Christian' and 'secular'. The Bible makes no distinctions between the two. I say to people that, quite simply, there's good and there's bad music, helpful music and not very helpful, and neutral music.

> *'Everything is permissible' – but not everything is beneficial.*
> *'Everything is permissible' – but not everything is constructive.*
> 1 Corinthians 10:23

I've had a few arguments with people about this over the years, and the lengths that people go to are quite amazing! How can an instrumental piece of music be Christian or non-Christian? A lot of dance music is instrumental, and it's useful sometimes to have no words and just allow people to dance and reach God through what's happening.

People go to ridiculous lengths to try to prove that secular music is dangerous, and really the argument goes nowhere. They say, 'Well, maybe it's the samples they use in the track,' or 'Maybe it's the drums.' But the fact is that most drum samples are made in a studio by a technician, and if you use a one-second drum sample recorded for Yamaha, it doesn't mean that it's not 'Christian music' you're creating.

My friend Kenny (who's a DJ in New York) simply says, 'Is your car Christian or non-Christian?' People answer, 'Well, it's just my car . . .' – and he says, 'Well, it's just my music . . .' It's as simple as that! If we can get rid of this false divide, then I believe Christians will impact society in a much more meaningful way.

Guerrilla warfare

Christians have made attempts to get into the music charts over the years. They want to get out there, get a Christian song in the charts and make an impact with a three-minute slot in the Top-40. But all this does is strengthen the sacred/secular divide: 'Let's run out of the bushes, throw a few holy-song hand grenades, and then run back into the safety of our nice Christian ghetto.'

We need to get an understanding of how God wants us to live in society, where there's a blurring of the boundaries between the sacred and secular. Real evangelism happens in youth groups where Christians and non-Christians interact together normally. Some people are scared of 'contamination', especially when it comes to young people. When I was a youth worker I have had conversations with well-meaning Christian parents around the issue of contamination by the big bad world. Yes, the world does have major problems, and things that will tempt us, and some people will fall away. But what we need to do is train ourselves fully for the battle – discipline ourselves so that we can live in society and still be a credible witness. But most importantly, we need to stay in society, and not get into the guerrilla warfare mentality.

I was at a wedding recently, and it was one of those full-day affairs which went on into the early hours of the morning. It was great to meet some of my old friends and find out what had been happening in their lives. (And it was sad in many ways to see what had not been happening in their lives, if you know what I mean.) We were staying in the hotel without the kids, and didn't have to drive anywhere, so I had a drink and just took things easy. (I'm not even going to enter into the discussion on whether Christians should drink or not. That's completely up to you – get over it.)

I quite enjoy relaxing with my friends and a beer. What happened at the wedding was that as the evening went on, people got steadily more and more drunk, but I was taking it steady and was quite happy just to relax with them. Maybe I winced at one or two of the jokes now and again, but I was happy to be in that culture, just being myself.

Jesus went to parties and was holy in some very difficult places, even with people who were out to kill him. In those times, a wedding was probably more than a one-day event, and I'm sure people got very drunk, but Jesus remained holy in these places, and I think we need to follow that model where we can.

John Drane (head of practical theology at the University of Aberdeen) went to a New Age fair and set up a stall called 'The Secret of the Tarot'. He did some research into tarot cards and found out that most are of biblical symbols, scenes and people, so what he did was allow people to come to his stall, show them the cards, and explain to them what the cards actually meant and how they pointed to Jesus.

Now some people reading this will be putting pen to paper to complain, but I listened to this guy and I was fascinated that he didn't see the New Age movement as a threat, but as a great opportunity to talk about Jesus to people in society who are open spiritually. I was so excited to hear what a radical man he was, being salt and light in one of the most difficult environments possible. Of course, for most men, going into a brothel would not be a good idea, and they may not be salt and light in that situation! We must use our common sense in these things, as John Drane did. He was wise and radical – a great combination.

Sink or swim

Maybe our discipleship techniques need to be looked at. I've been so excited to see some radical youth groups discipling young people to live in the world. It's like learning to swim

– some people learn to swim in a swimming pool, which is great, but once you start swimming in the ocean, it's a completely different environment, because the sea is real and the swimming pool isn't. Maybe our discipleship goes as far as teaching people to swim well in the swimming pool, but not against strong currents and against the waves in the ocean. Over the last few years I've seen friends of mine I thought could swim well, but who have drowned in the culture of the world and are not following Jesus any more – which is gutting, but maybe inevitable, at least for some.

I have been tempted in many different ways, and I believe that people can choose not to fall away from Jesus. People can talk about it, they can theologize it, or whatever they want, but it's a choice. Are you choosing to fall away from Jesus? It's about knowing your boundaries; knowing how far you can handle things. I think it's obvious that we do have to run away from things sometimes, but other times we need to stop and to take control of our thoughts and our actions.

The weapons we fight with are not the weapons of the world. On the contrary, they have divine power to demolish strongholds. We demolish arguments and every pretension that sets itself up against the knowledge of God, and we take captive every thought to make it obedient to Christ.
2 Corinthians 10:4–5

Accountability

There's been a lot of talk about accountability over the last few years. Some people don't really understand what it is. I'm trying to learn myself. People are very happy to be 'accountable' until someone wants to hold them to account! When you're doing something wrong, and you're in an accountable relationship with someone you trust, then that person needs to say, 'Well, actually that's out of order,' and you need to say, 'Yes, I understand that it's not right, and I will try not to do that again. Help me to do this.' That is what accountability is. It's not 'heavy shepherding', it's not heavy leadership – it's respecting somebody and allowing them to have input into your life, your temptations and your struggles. It's an inner circle

That's how we survive in the world.

That's how we choose not to fall.

A simple way to develop a real, accountable relationship is to ask someone you respect, who is the same sex as you, to meet with you on a regular basis. Get them to ask you about the three main things you struggle with – it could be spending too much money, late-night TV, or your relationship with your girlfriend or wife.

This world is not your home, so don't make yourselves cozy in it. Don't indulge your ego at the expense of your soul. Live an exemplary life among the natives so that your actions will refute their prejudices. Then they'll be won over to God's side and be there to join in the celebration when he arrives. Make the Master proud of you by being good citizens.
1 Peter 2:11–13, *The Message*

Nearly everywhere I go and speak, whether it's to men or not, I always say, 'You must have non-Christian friends', or friends who are 'not yet Christians' (as they say now in a PC kind of way). I'd go so far as to say that if you don't have friends who are not Christians, then you're probably not following Jesus properly.[34]

We need to be party people

I am convinced that religion's historic concerns for dogma, orthodoxy, tradition, hierarchy, order and good taste are quite foreign to anything Jesus taught. He had deeper quests in mind – namely, touching the broken-hearted, healing the sick, welcoming the outcast, casting out demons, humbling the powerful, lifting up the lowly, feeding the hungry, releasing captives and giving sight to the blind. In pursuit of his quests, he brought people together and forged relationships. Our ritualized re-enactments of the Last Supper, whose every detail we have fought over and fine-tuned, fail to capture the radical and messy spirit of what Jesus himself did. My advice to pastors who dare to be effective is: throw lots of parties, get to know your flock, and then serve and preach to them as friends. Be ready for trouble, for when deepening relationships yield change, the agent of change will come under assault. My advice to lay leaders is: cut council meetings short, spend less time and heat on financial management, and instead bring food to the parties, embrace the new and overlooked, and protect the pastor when relationship-building bears the fruit of vitality and growth. My advice to evangelism teams is: skip the brochures, ads, telemarketing, follow-up cards and other easy stuff, and instead invite people to dinner.[35]

We need to do what we can – have fun, tell jokes, dance (if you can!), but most of all let's be ourselves instead of grey-faced religious segregationists. Embarrass yourself occasionally! Have a laugh – it's OK, honest! That's how people will know that we are different.

Living out this theology would empower and release inactive believers. There are millions who sense that the only way they can serve God is to sit there like good little church members and hope they make it into small group leadership!
Roger Ellis & Chris Seaton[36]

The earth is the Lord's, and everything in it, the world, and all who live in it.
Psalm 24:1

The whole of the world belongs to God. Doesn't that give us a great opportunity to be part of the world as active members, instead of always complaining about it, making attacks into the enemy camp and then running back into the safety of our church worship and tea rotas?

Questions

- What divides have you heard implied in church?
- Is there anything that God cannot use for his purposes?
- Are we scared of contamination?
- How do we avoid a guerrilla-warfare mentality?
- How practical is being holy?
- What are your experiences of accountable relationships?
- Are you actually accountable to anyone?
- If we call something secular, are we saying that God cannot affect it? What does that do to God?

Most of us women like men, you know; it's just that we find them a constant disappointment.

Attributed to Clare Short, MP

13

You are Odd!

Baz

Did you know that pi is one of the most important mathematical constants, approximately equal to 3.14159? It represents the ratio of any circle's circumference to its diameter in Euclidean geometry, which is the same as the ratio of a circle's area to the square of its radius.

Of course you did. Yeah, right! I have always been crap at maths – or math, for our friends over the pond. You say, 'Tomato', we say, 'Tomato'. Anyway, back to the point. At school, from an early age, I struggled learning my times tables and anything else to do with maths.

I remember vividly, at the age of 14 in a maths lesson, being asked by my teacher, Mr Walker, if I understood the algebraic formula he had just shown us all on the blackboard.[37] After his fourth attempt to show me how to work out the formula, he became very frustrated and animated, and just threw the board-rubber at me and said, 'Get up and go next door!'

The Litter Bin

If you were sent next door to Mr Harrison's class, you knew what the punishment was. It was the dreaded litter bin. You had to get inside it and just stand there for the rest of the lesson whilst he continued to teach.

So knocking on Mr H's door, I was called in and was asked what I wanted.

'Mr Walker has sent me, sir.'

'Oh, well, you know what to do, Gascoyne.'

'Yes, sir.' I walked towards the bin and stepped inside as the giggles began to intensify.

Fortunately, that did help me with my maths, as I just decided that I was crap at it and would always be crap at it. And every year, after we had taken our maths exam, we would have to sit through the ordeal of having our exam results read out in front of the whole class. We had 34 pupils in the class, so it would go something like this:

'In first place, Johnson, with 87 per cent. Well done, Johnson. In second place, with 85 per cent, Andrews. Good result' – and so on, until I and three other lonely, vulnerable pupils were waiting for their names to be called out and their results to be proclaimed for all to hear. Eventually: 'Gascoyne, in 33rd position, 13 per cent.' *I did it!* I thought. *I did not come last this time!* But I always did end up in the last three. Consistent was my middle name!

Seven years ago I decided to try to do GCSE maths, and every Tuesday evening I went to learn why $y + 5 = 12$ and what the nth term was. Why? Because I wanted to prove to others and myself that I was not thick or useless. Each week I struggled, especially when the lecturer would explain something and write down different formulas for us to learn so we could then solve the different problems given to us.

Each week I would go through the same discussion with the lecturer: 'Please could you tell me who came up with this formula and how and why, as this will help me then understand how to do the work.'

Every week the same response: 'You don't need to know that, Baz – just do the work.'

'No, you don't understand. I do need to know, as this is how my brain works. Once I know why and who, then I find I can do the how, but not until then.'

Due to my frustration at not being able to understand and my fear of failing the exam, I quit the course six weeks before the final exam.

So, I still struggle with numbers, whether it be when I sit down with my wife and try to go over our finances, or when I play golf and try to mark my card whilst playing the Stableford Rules. Sorry if you are not into golf, but Stableford is a way of scoring golf so that all the golfers, no matter how good, play off a 'level playing field', and you mark your cards according to your 'handicap'. I have no idea how this works and cannot do it when playing and feel more inadequate each time I play.

Dyslexia

Well, that was until the beginning of this year, when I went for a free dyslexia test. I had to fight the feelings of embarrassment, fear, frustration and stupidity as I waited for the test to begin. Sharon, the young lady who did my test, was very friendly and reassuring and quickly helped me lay aside my fears. After all the tests and feedback from Sharon, it was obvious that my brain does not function well with numbers.

Sharon did actually say in a very kind and non-judgemental way, 'Has anyone ever said you are odd?'

I laughed and replied, 'Many times, especially within the church! Why do you ask?'

'Well, in all the tests we do, usually two tests show us immediately if a person is dyslexic. Well, in the first test you did amazingly well and scored off the chart, and you are really good academically. But in the other test we do, with numbers, your score was really low, and this does show you have a problem with numeracy.'

I can't tell you how releasing this was, and reassuring!

Whilst she was just working out my final scores, she gave me about ten different-coloured gels to look through whilst reading a book, to see if this would help me at all. Some of the colours did not improve my ability to see the words or register them in my brain. But when I placed the yellow, green or blue gels over the words on the page, it was like someone had turned a light on inside my brain. The words were no bigger on the page, but somehow inside my head they seemed massive and it was like they were registering in my memory.

I have always struggled with short-term memory. My long-term memory is fantastic. I can remember my first day at school, the teacher's name, the names of the pupils and what we did – no problem. But ask me what I had just read on a page of a book, and my mind would go blank. I would need to read the page over and over again to get anything to sink in and stay in. It seems that with these different-coloured gels, my memory is improving and I am seeing things differently.

How many men have been told they are useless because they could not understand maths or something else, when there is a simple solution to the problem?

Three days after discovering that I had an issue with dyslexia, I was at a leaders' conference for the network that my church relates to. A man called Dave came up to me. I had known him for over twenty years but could not really call him a close friend.

He said, 'Baz, before this conference I was thinking about you, and I think God wants me to say you are odd.'

Odd! Did I hear right?

'Say what, Dave?'

'You are odd, and this is a good thing, as you see things differently to others, and we need this in the church.'

I was reminded of the conversation only three days earlier whilst having my dyslexia test: 'Has anyone ever told you are odd?' Well, here God was telling me the same thing through Dave.

God is really brilliant at getting our attention, and once he has got it, he can then get over what he wants to say to us.

He had my attention all right, and I was able to receive his encouraging words from Dave. I had always felt odd before I became a follower of Jesus, and then so much more when I said 'Yes' to Jesus and became one of his disciples, as I have always struggled to feel that I fit into the church.

Being odd is not the problem; not believing that you and I are unique is the problem. When I decided to follow Jesus, someone gave me the following verse: 'You didn't choose me but I chose you to bear fruit, fruit that will last.' I thought, *That's nice.* It is only in the last year that I have discovered what Jesus meant when he said that to his followers and what it means today for us. It means he believes in us, and we can become the people that God intended us to be. Please check out the Rob Bell DVD *Dust* (part of the *Nooma* series) and watch it as many times as it takes for the truth to sink into your heart, mind and soul, because it's so releasing.

Just as I now see things differently through my coloured gels when I am reading, I am seeing that God sees me differently to the way I see myself.

No longer in the litter bin, feeling like rubbish!

I am a unique and loved individual with so much potential and influence – and so are you.

We act as though comfort and luxury were the chief requirements of life, when all we need to make us really happy is something to be enthusiastic about.

Charles Kingsley (1819–75)

14

The Career Magnet

Lee

It's true that most of us, as we are growing up, think that our dads don't understand much, but there are a few things I remember my dad telling me as we discussed life, the universe, and everything. One of the things he told me was that Christians are always radical until they have 'their button pushed by God'. Full-on, born-again, singing and dancing, radical Christians may sink back for several reasons – the main ones being money, status, family and career.

The 'career-magnet' has amazing power over men; it will soon take over if given half a chance. I believe that every single one of us lives by faith, whether we have a lot of money or no money at all. But somehow, when someone has a job which pays bills very well and becomes a 'career', they can seem to lose their faith in God and place more faith in their job. Their whole being, existence, status, self-esteem and self-image are all connected to their job. This is scary, especially since we are all two pay-cheques away from the homeless shelter. I suppose we should ask, 'Where is our security?'

You are not your job.
From the film *Fight Club*[38]

A job for life

The world of work is changing rapidly. When I was in the civil service – before most of it became privatized agencies – it was literally a job for life, and I worked with people who had been there for forty years or more and were just waiting for retirement – they were 'unsackable'. They knew the system well and did just enough to scrape by, while making the rest of us miserable! I got so fed up with the moaning of one colleague one day that I said to her, 'Why don't you just leave?' I felt like a stranger walking into a Wild West saloon! I am sure I saw tumbleweed going past the door.

Now the world of work has changed. People are often under threat of redundancy on a monthly basis. They are consultants and contractors who work for short periods of time, always hoping that the contract will be renewed again. This really puts the pressure on Christians to question where their security lies. Yosser Hughes, in the gritty eighties drama *The Boys from the Black Stuff*, was a symbol of how a job is often the man, as he fell into a meltdown after being made redundant. The threat of redundancy is, I believe, one of the things that really strikes fear deep into men's hearts, especially if they have a family, or need to support a large house or an expensive car. It's as if their whole life is on the line.

Please don't misunderstand me – I'm not into so-called 'Christian' and 'non-Christian' jobs, I just believe there are different ways to serve God. Some people really do serve God well in their chosen career. My friends John and Fiona are both career-minded people, and it's interesting to hear their struggles and anxieties as we have prayed that they would be great followers of Jesus in their work environment. I find it difficult as well when young people don't want to serve God, or more often, are not allowed to serve God in short-term missions or training. I've seen some excellent Christian young people whose parents have put enormous pressure on them not to take a 'year out', because they want their children to get a 'decent' job. In this way, parents teach their kids that serving God isn't a proper job – no wonder we are in a mess. Most parents ask their children, 'What are you going to do when you grow up?' Something with status is always desirable, such as a doctor or solicitor, especially in middle-class environments – which is, frankly, most of the church in the UK.

Fathers send their children to college either because they went to college, or because they did not.
L. L. Hendren

Hiding

Another issue not talked about much is 'hiding' in your job. I've certainly been guilty of this myself. A friend of mine who is a manager and deals with overtime is absolutely convinced that many of the men who work for her deliberately take overtime so they don't have to spend time with their families. If they don't want to attend something – a family gathering or event – that is when they'll say, 'Sorry, I'm working.' If you say, 'Actually, I quite fancy staying at home' or 'I'm seeing my wife tonight', then people will question you, but not if you say you are working. Funny, that.

Some men hide from their families, from real relationships, and they use their jobs as a place where they don't have to be Dad and they don't have to be sharing the TV remote control with somebody else. We have to ask ourselves – have we been guilty of hiding in our jobs in the past? Are we doing that now?

Do we work longer than we have to? I could busy myself in my job and keep myself there all night if I wanted to, but those things aren't so important that I must miss seeing my kids before they go to bed.

It's amazing the games we play with ourselves, in our minds and with our families, and how easily we can use our jobs to hide from things we don't want to face. This is often seen in so-called 'ministry' as, of course, leading a church or mission organization is an endless task.

Remember: if you win the rat race – you are still a rat!
Anonymous

I once played basketball with a guy who worked seven days a week, and he was the most miserable man I had ever met. I think he actually enjoyed it in a strange sort of way. Of course there are financial pressures, but taking a day off will help us to do our jobs better in the other five or six days anyway. I think the Bible may mention it – mmmm . . . I know for myself, that after a while at work I may be there but I'm not really doing the job very well, and I believe Jesus asks us to do everything to the best of our ability. Even a day away from email can make a big difference.

Unless the job means more than the pay, it will never pay more.
Attributed to H. Bertram Lewis

The financial decisions we make can also become a trap. We get a good job, we buy a big house, we get a better car, and we make the decision sometimes to send our kids to private school. This can then affect the rest of our lives because we feel we have to keep the kids in that school, we have to keep a house that size, and we need to have a big car, and so on. And those things become the excuse that drives us to the Catch-22 situation that distorted careers can bring.

Following Jesus

Being a Christian, as you know, is just simply following Jesus, and in following him we have to talk to him and ask him what he wants. As we become more like him, we don't need to spend hours in prayer trying to make a small decision, because we know what he would think about it. The financial decisions we make, often done in good heart, do have big repercussions on our priorities, and if we're not very careful they can drive us away from being Christ-like in all aspects. These are the practical things that Jesus is interested in – how we live our life, and how we actually follow him. I know most men's desire is to provide for their family, and that's a good and right thing – but we must have God in the equation. We can't do it alone. Being self-employed amplifies this one, I know!

Clare and I have often been short of money because we often didn't bring much in, and being a DJ and having twins puts a lot of pressure on us financially. I believe I'm taking a more practical view on lots of things now. Once I did some extra basketball coaching for the council, which paid quite well, and that was a good use of my time, but I also need to have my faith mixed into that too. I need to pray that God will provide the things that we need, as well as doing things practically for myself. Some people are called to live by faith completely, which means relying on God for everything, with no income. Others – like me – work and have 'faith' as well. It's about finding the balance and finding our trust in God through the whole thing.

Just in the last few weeks, while re-writing this chapter, I have made some big decisions about my working life. It's a good season for us, and we have relied on God a little more, as sometimes I don't earn enough to live on. But God helps us and we don't go without the essentials. But the most important bit is that God, not my career, is first right now – and that is a daily battle I have to remind myself of.

> *The things you own, can end up owning you.*
> Anonymous

The man with everything

I spoke to a guy called 'Douglas' recently and he had everything that he wanted. He could have followed in his father's footsteps into a multi-million-pound business. He had a mobile when no one else had one, a sports car, all the women he wanted, everything materially that he wanted – but he said he got to a point where he was suddenly aware that he really needed God. Even though in the world's eyes he 'wanted for nothing', he still had an enormous desire and massive need for God.

So the whole idea of how our life would be sorted out if we won the lottery is a lie, because unless we submit our careers and our lives wholly to God, then we will never truly follow our heart, and we will never really be living. Douglas said he had to leave his job to live in a run-down house with a few lads who were on fire for Jesus before he started to live. God sorted him out and also brought him the woman who will continue to sort him out! As we talked, we agreed that actually, materialism is nothing to do with how much money you've got; it's an attitude of heart. You can be living on benefits and be extremely materialistic, or you can have a million pounds and not be.

Being busy is not necessarily a sign of success either. A friend of mine taught me a lesson in how to live my life. Paul is a real success in the world's eyes – a single young dentist, and popular with the ladies. But as I talked to him about his work, I realized he has made some great decisions. He works just four days a week, and he chooses not to do the work that brings in the most money – he likes to meet real people. He has a balanced life and has made godly decisions, even though he is not a Christian right now. He seems more sorted than a lot of Christians I know!

*Don't become so well-adjusted to your culture that you fit into it
without even thinking. Instead, fix your attention on God.*
Romans 12:2, *The Message*

Questions for groups

- Do we put too much value on being busy?
- What is a 'proper job'?
- Is there a difference between a job and a career?
- Do you hide in your job?
- What cultural aspects of work put pressure on you in the light of Romans 12:2?
- What would happen if you were made redundant?
- Has the recession changed your outlook?

Going deeper

The Celtic Christians had an amazing understanding of God's creation and would often talk about the flow of the tides as their philosophy on living their lives. Roger Ellis and Chris Seaton write:

> The worldview of the Celts was remarkably holistic . . . passionate, adventurous and full of wandering, their Eastern-influenced spirituality also gave them a great appetite for meditation, Scripture and seeking God. It is this unique spiritual 'genetic code', reflected in our aboriginal apostles, which resonates so strongly with us today.[39]

At Lindisfarne, now known as Holy Island (the place where indigenous Christianity started in England), one of my favourite places is St Cuthbert's Island, which is a few hundred yards off the beach and only accessible for a few hours a day. St

Cuthbert was a great character – he once spent the night waist deep in the sea in order to stay awake to pray! He used to go there because he knew he needed uninterrupted time with God. When the tide was in he could not get back to land; it was just him, his lantern and God. David Adam says:

> Cuthbert, very like tidal Holy Island, recognized the need for rhythm in life. It cannot be all open, or all closed. Life needs a balance. Sometimes we need to be very much part of the mainland and all that is going on; at other times we need to be an island for a while. We all need space, a time set apart, free from noise and busyness. If we cannot find an island we need to create one. Perpetual busyness is a great danger to the life of the spirit.[40]

Questions

- Do we need a sense of the ebb and flow of the tides in our life?
- How does technology help or hinder us in this quest?
- Why do people burn out?
- Do you know people who need to slow down?
- If we keep pushing, what happens?
- What did Jesus teach us about the ebb and flow?

I would rather trust a woman's instinct than a man's reason.

Stanley Baldwin (1867–1947)

15

Never on a Sunday

Baz

More and more people are going to their church on a Sunday rather than ours. Whether it be a DIY superstore, a coffee shop or to watch football, we need to realize that Sundays are no longer sacred. Let's get over it and use the opportunities and allow our sacred cow to die.

Ever since my fifth birthday, sport has been a passion of mine. Memories of my first football and football boots are still vivid. I would spend hours in the cobbled back alley kicking a football against the wall and dreaming of the day when I would become a professional footballer. At the age of 11, I had the privilege of playing in a cup final at Darlington Football Club ground, again reinforcing what I wanted to do when I left school.

Senior school introduced me to so many sports: athletics, basketball, cricket, football, rugby, softball, swimming and volleyball became part of my weekly sporting diet. In the classroom I felt insecure and incapable of achieving, but outside I felt free – able to excel at something.

At the age of 15, I had a trial for a professional football club. Was my dream about to become a reality? The answer was a big NO! On the third day at the club, while I was doing some physical training, the player coach sexually interfered with me. Confused and angry, I left the club without saying anything to anyone. My dream had been snatched away before I had been given a proper chance to give it my best shot.

I struggled with the comments from friends and family, offering me their advice for the future, when they were oblivious to what had happened. I did not dare tell my mother, as she is built like Pat from *EastEnders* and would probably have gone with a pair of pliers to castrate the guy! My mates would just have found something amusing to say about it.

I continued to play sports, especially football and rugby. My behaviour on the field became more aggressive and erratic, as I struggled with what had happened.

Priorities

Something else I struggled with was the issue of priorities. In a Christian magazine I once read an article entitled 'Sunday – A Day to Pray or Play'. It was about a young boy named Samson and his parents, and the tension caused by Samson's desire to play football on a Sunday rather than go to church. On occasions his parents would physically escort him to church. Samson's mother was quoted as saying, 'I am so upset Samson has chosen football over the Lord. We are a God-fearing family who do not expect this to be the case.'[41]

I need to say at this point that I am not a parent yet so I do not know how Christian parents feel when this problem arises. However, I do believe that children, teenagers and adults are not usually choosing between sport and God but between sport and the church. And in most cases there is no contest – sport wins hands down! Why? Maybe because church is not relevant for these people and they get their love, support and encouragement from their sporting colleagues. To them, sport is their church.

One of the things I struggled with more than anything else when I became a Christian was the way a few people made it clear that they were not happy with me playing sport if it interfered with church attendance. This became a huge problem for me, as football was such a large part of my life. I loved playing the game, but also needed the friendships I had acquired over the years through football. What was God's view on this? Did he want me to stop or continue, with his help, to show my friends the difference he had made to my life? Surely this was better than packing the game in and isolating myself from them by being consumed into the Christian ghetto.

One of my friends, who attended the same church, decided to help me with witnessing to my football colleagues. He bought me a sew-on cotton badge for the front of my football shirt, with the words 'Jesus is my Lord'. He said it would give me plenty of opportunities to talk about my faith in God. So, as a naïve teenager eager to do the right thing, I asked my grandmother to sew it on for me. My friend was right. It gave me plenty of opportunities – to be embarrassed and receive a barrage of obscenities and sarcasm! Every week I would hear the same phrases repeated: 'It's Bible-basher Baz'; 'There's Moses'; 'Gascoyne has got religion'; and some were not repeatable. The biggest challenge for me became how quickly I could cover the badge with mud after leaving the changing room. This only increased my sense of guilt and condemnation, feeling I was letting God down by being a poor witness.

I remember that once I needed to go to the loo before we kicked off at a match I was playing in. As there were no toilets around, I just went behind the goal to relieve myself. As I was doing this, my manager John shouted over to me, 'Call yourself a Christian, doing that!'

I looked over at him in amazement – which was a mistake, as I peed on my leg and socks. After the match I asked my manager what he had meant by his comment. He thought that now that I was a Christian, I would not want to do the same as the rest of the players. We had a laugh together when I replied, 'Christians still need to go to the toilet, just like anyone else.'

After that incident John and I got on really well. Later that year his youngest son died, and we were able to have some deep talks together. He asked me to pray for his wife, his children and himself. I believe that came about from just being myself and trying to show something of God's love in the way I trained, played and befriended the other guys, despite all the banter because of my faith.

I wish I could say that I have always been a good example on the football pitch and never let myself or God down. I used to play for three different teams during the weekend, on Saturday afternoon, Sunday morning and Sunday afternoon. The team I played for on Saturday had the highest standard of football but it was also the area where I got into the most trouble. There was one person I played against who was five years older than me. Every time we played, he would start a fight with me. I would ask God to help me show something of God's love to him, by not reacting or retaliating when he fouled me deliberately or punched me when the referee was not looking.

I would usually manage this, but then at one match I failed big time. I had just received the ball with my back to the goal when this guy came flying in to tackle me and took both my legs away from under me with no intention of trying to get the ball. I could feel the anger rising as I slowly tried to get up. I thought to myself, *OK, God, I apologize now for what I am going to do!*

As I got up I stretched out one of my legs. I knew this guy was still behind me and I caught him right in the throat with my boot. Still not looking back, I slowly jogged away, running off my injury, pretending I didn't know what had happened. When I eventually looked round, this guy was lying on the grass, receiving some assistance from their coach.

I remember talking to my youth leader about how I didn't want to lose my temper while playing football or mess up any opportunities of witnessing. Bill just told me to apologize when I did wrong but said, 'Don't allow yourself to be walked all over just because people think you are going to be a soft touch because of your new-found faith.'

I only played for the Sunday morning team when the first-choice keeper was away or injured. I played in goal as my second position, only because no one else was daft enough to do it. At the end of one season I was asked to play the final game. Whoever won this won the league. Our opponents had a few ex-professionals in their team and were favourites to win. It's amazing how pumped up you can get when someone tells you your team isn't expected to win.

One of the opponents I was not pleased to see was a guy who had deliberately broken my ankle three years previously. Unfortunately, ten minutes into the game, I made a mistake from which they scored. There must have been about seventy-five people watching this match, all shouting their opinions.

Fortunately, with thirty minutes to go, we scored to equalize. From then on the tempo increased. I came out to intercept a pass that had been put through to one of their forwards. As I picked the ball up, the forward followed through with his boot and caught me on the leg. As I stood there looking at him, he swore at me and punched me in the face.

Chin him!

Immediately there was a shout from the touch-line from a few of my friends: 'Chin him, Baz!' (meaning punch him back). It was just like my brain went into autopilot, and the next thing I knew, my fist had made contact with his face and he was lying on the grass.

Immediately I thought of the 'Jesus is my Lord' badge on my shirt, so I pulled the ball up to my chest as the referee approached. I was waiting to be sent off when he just told us both to grow up and get on with the game.

The match ended in a draw. At the end of the match I went up to the forward and apologized for what I had done. I explained I had become a Christian and should not have reacted like that. His response was, 'It's OK, mate. I deserved it.'

Because of the draw, we had to play a replay the following Tuesday. As the keeper was on holiday, I played in that match as well. The match was more physical than the previous one, and I asked God to help me play to the best of my ability and not lose my temper. Both prayers were answered. We finished 4–2 and won the league. The victory was made even sweeter when we discovered that our opponents were on £50 per man and we were on a pint of whatever we wanted from the local club.

I tell you those two stories just to emphasize the pressure and the problems that can arise for Christian men, young or old, while taking part in a competitive sport. I do believe that Christianity and competitive sports are compatible. However, we need to be honest about our struggles and make sure we allow God into this area of our lives. Sport is a fantastic way of getting alongside people, whether it's during training, playing a match, a round of golf or just watching. Whatever your interest – playing, coaching or watching – remember to enjoy it to the full and allow God to use you, your gift and the forum he has given to you. A book I would highly recommend is *What the Book Says About Sport* by Stuart Weir from Christians in Sport.

Questions

- Is winning the most important thing to you?
- Do you have a problem controlling your anger while playing? What are you doing about it?
- If you do have a problem in this way, would it be wise to give up playing your sport for a while?
- Has your church ever thought about doing a sports day as an outreach? How could you help organize this?
- Is it wrong for Christians to defend themselves while playing a sport, or should they turn the other cheek?
- How far would you go to win? Would you cheat or break the rules? Would you injure someone else for your cause?

- Should Christian men be involved in playing sports on a Sunday?
- Is it true that most Christian football leagues are worse for disciplinary actions than other leagues?
- Can you lose a game and still enjoy your sport?

Integrity is so perishable in the summer months of success.

Vanessa Redgrave

16

Keep On Keeping On

Lee

Writing about longevity and tenacity in an increasingly temporary world is always good fun. 'A job for life' doesn't exist any more, and when our TV breaks we throw it away without even thinking about getting it fixed. Even authors of men's books who talk about the long haul sometimes don't make it[42] – scary stuff. In a world that's getting faster, what can we learn from digging our heels in?

Youth workers often stay in their job for only two to three years, or so statistics say. When things get difficult, or life is pressured, it's often easier to move on – and this is a struggle that I've dealt with over the last few years.

I was a schools worker in Leeds for fourteen years. Leeds is a place where I want to be, and where my wife and I are going to stay unless we get a signed postcard from God telling us otherwise. This flies in the face of traditional youth work, where you go and do your stuff for a couple of years and then you can move on. And actually, as Paul Borthwick pointed out, the sadness of this is that you can have three years' worth of good ideas, then when you run out, you can always go somewhere else and use those ideas again. So twenty years down the road, you're still trying out the same ideas you had twenty years ago. This is an easy thing to slip into as a youth worker, especially as you've got to be inspired and an ideas-driven kind of person.

Warfare

But what is getting me excited more than anything else at the moment is people who just say: 'God's called me here, and I'm staying!' Just standing still is sometimes warfare – never mind moving forward. 'What we've got, we'll keep', as the Second World War posters used to say. It may be a lot more exciting to travel the world and go to different places. However, that has never had the same attraction for me as staying where I am and seeing God transform the place where I live.

And thankfully, in Leeds there are a lot of people who feel the same way, and we're here to see this through as long as we can. I have the privilege of being with people who have been here for thirty years or more, and are still watching for God to move in the city of Leeds.

Our friend Martin says, 'This is a bad time to give up.' You may think this is obvious, but it is very good advice. This is a bad time to give up, because you haven't seen it through. You haven't seen what God has yet to do. It's always a bad time to give up!

In George Otis Jrs book *Transformations* he states that in all cases of God transforming a community, there are two common factors: persevering leadership and fervent, informed prayer. We must learn to fuel the fire within us (or maybe just light it!).

Our goal is unashamedly territorial. It is to see the will of God expressed in a particular patch of earth. We will not be vague in our praying, but focused, looking for the coming of the kingdom where we are. We will seek God for revelation about what is hindering the coming of that kingdom, with the full awareness that he gives revelation in proportion to what we can affect.
Martin Scott[43]

I'm not saying we shouldn't have travelling missions groups and itinerant ministries. But these people should not be the norm; surely we should see the majority of people staying where they are, praying and trying to make a difference.

I have a friend who is extremely gifted – certainly more gifted than I am in many areas. But the shame is that over the last few years I have seen him move from place to place, and I just wonder what he has achieved and what moves him on.

People might not be excited about me being here in Leeds for fourteen years, working with the same young people and schools, but I think that God's heart is to dig deep and get your hands dirty. The deeper you dig, the harder it gets, but the closer you are. Maybe the secret is to stay and get more passionate, and not to move on when the passion wears out.

The good influence of godly citizens causes a city to prosper, but the moral decay of the wicked drives it downhill.
Proverbs 11:11, TLB

Test of faith

I was once involved in a really big church event in Leeds in which I was the compère. It was there that I had one of the strangest experiences of my life, which really affected me. I spent the previous two weeks talking at a youth celebration in Leeds about the cost of discipleship and the fact that people give their lives for Jesus all the time in other countries, and, as Ed Silvoso says, maybe it's time to reclaim that gift of martyrdom. So there I was, right in the centre of Leeds, right in the hub of the city, leading this celebration, and I suddenly had the fear that I might lose my life there and then. I suddenly thought, all it takes is one person to make a mistake, to do something stupid, or intentional, and that could be it for me in this public arena. And for a whole week afterwards, this totally wiped me out. It was the first thing I thought about in the morning, and the last thing I thought about at night. Bizarre!

A few years ago, my friend Justin and I were rehearsing our song 'Jumping in the House of God' with The Tribe at the 'Event for Revival' in Norfolk. It was an afternoon rehearsal and sound-check. All five of us were rapping together, and all of a sudden, out of nowhere, this man appeared with fists flying. He attacked me and Mark Pennels, grabbed Justin's microphone, and used it to hit him on the jaw. He hit him so hard that Justin had the imprint of the microphone on his cheek for a couple of days afterwards! Obviously the noise had been too much for him. I think he had been camping nearby and he just flipped, and that was it! We had to sit on him in the end to calm him down and try to find the people he was with. There were stewards and security people there, but it still happened. Says a lot for nice Christian event security!

Whenever you do anything publicly, you always leave yourself open to people with strange ideas, or even psychiatric problems that may spark them off to do something crazy. It's funny, but in those times your faith is put to the test. Those are the times when you realize what you do and don't believe. A lot of Western Christians have never had the opportunity to have their faith tested, so they probably don't know what to believe, or worst of all, they are just apathetic or not particularly bothered. Apathy has almost killed the Western church.

Staying where you are and digging in where God's called you is to experience something of the heart of God. God is faithful, and we should be too. It's as simple as that. We should not be people who move endlessly on from one thing to another.

I learnt very quickly during my time with Youth With A Mission that you make where you are, your home. Even in the five months that I was there, we carried photographs and personal belongings around with us, and wherever we were that night, we used to put up photographs to make it home and not have the view that we were just drifting through. Wherever I am, whether it's for years or for days, I try to make my home there and make the most of it.

Apathy has almost killed the Western Church.

God likes to work things out through people and relationships. This is where our reality kicks in, because our faith in God is tested in difficult and day-to-day situations. God roots us in people and in places. His character is not fly-by-night. If you want an example of this, look at the people of Israel in Exodus. Why was God so faithful to Israel when they wandered around the desert in circles? Why was he so faithful to them when they made images of idols while Moses met with God (Exod. 32)? It's because it's in God's nature. He's here for the long term, for the long haul. He's beyond time anyway, so it makes no difference to him! He wants us to dig in.

I worked in the same schools for years, which was longer than a lot of the staff because of the high turnover rate. At least I couldn't be accused of being a mad proselytizing evangelist, because I was there week after week. God blessed me and showed me his faithfulness, and I found people were more open to God when they saw I was there for them for the long term.

Once a teacher in a school gave me a Technics 1210 turntable worth about £250 for my DJ work. He said, 'I want to give it to you in appreciation of all the work you've done in school.' He didn't fall on his knees and say, 'How can I be saved?' But he recognized that what I was doing in school was making a difference in people's lives.

Perseverance

Do not underestimate the gift of perseverance. When Steve Chalke was asked, 'What's your greatest gift?' he simply said, 'I think my greatest gift is that I'm a plodder. I just get on with it day by day – keep pushing it, keep doing it . . .'[44] That's exactly the sort of person I want to be. I make mistakes, but I keep plodding on and learning from my mistakes.

Sometimes being a Christian is an act of will, especially when heaven appears silent. You have to put your faith into action, and not just expect fluffy, nice feelings to come your way. The best way not to give up is just not to give up!

When Winston Churchill was invited back to his old school, it was a great moment for them all as the head teacher introduced one of the greatest public speakers and one of the most influential people of recent times. Churchill was given a huge build-up. He worked his way to the front of the stage in typical shuffling style, looked at the young men sitting before him and simply told them never to give up. Imagine the faces of the robed teachers, who had expected a mega-inspirational and very long speech! This man, with all his faults, had managed to capture something of the heart of God, and the perseverance we need in order to live out our lives.

We have instant gratification in our society: instant coffee, instant meals, instant everything. In fact we're not happy unless we've got at least 327 channels of repeats on TV to flick through at any one time. But some things are worth waiting for, and I'm waiting here in Leeds for the time that God promised.

In a study of the history of religion in Leeds, the introduction says, 'The most remarkable thing about the history of religion in Leeds is that nothing remarkable has ever happened!' (This is not strictly true, if you consider that Smith Wigglesworth had his first experience of miraculous healing here – but they ignored that.)

If you know you're going to be somewhere for the rest of your life, maybe you make each day count. This note was found in the office of a young pastor in Zimbabwe following his martyrdom for his faith in Jesus Christ:

I'm part of the fellowship of the unashamed. I have the Holy Spirit power. The die has been cast. I have stepped over the line. The decision has been made – I'm a disciple of his. I won't look back, let up, slow down, back away, or be still. My past is redeemed, my present makes sense, my future is secure. I'm finished and done with low living, sight walking, smooth knees, colourless dreams, tamed visions, worldly talking, cheap giving and dwarfed goals. I no longer need pre-eminence, prosperity, position, promotions, plaudits or popularity. I don't have to be right, first, tops, recognized, praised, regarded or rewarded. I now live by faith, lean in his presence, walk by patience, am uplifted by prayer, and I labour with power. My life is set, my gait is fast, my goal is heaven, my road is narrow, my way rough, my companions are few, my guide reliable, my mission clear. I cannot be bought, compromised, detoured, lured away, turned back, deluded or delayed. I will not flinch in the face of sacrifice, hesitate in the presence of the enemy, pander at the pool of popularity, or meander in the maze of mediocrity. I won't give up, shut up, let up, until I have stayed up, stored up, prayed up, paid up, preached up for the cause of Christ. I am a disciple of Jesus. I must go till he comes, give till I drop, preach till all know, and work till he stops me. And, when he comes for his own, he will have no problem recognizing me. My banner will be clear!

Questions

- Have you ever feared for your life?
- Why do our prayers for a place mean more if we are living there?
- Are you a 'three-year-move-on' type of bloke?
- What is drifting through? Are you doing it?
- What can you do this week to dig in deeper?

The man who lets himself be bored is even more contemptible than the bore.

Samuel Butler (1835–1902)

17

Walk the Plank!

Baz

God offends the mind to reveal what's in our hearts.
John Scotland[45]

I believe in the surprises of the Holy Spirit.
L.J. Stevens[46]

Some time ago I visited a friend who lives and works in Romania. He has been working with street children for over twelve years now and has seen God provide for this work in many amazing ways. I first had the privilege of visiting the work in 1999 and it was tremendous to go back and see how things had developed and to visit some of the children I had met before. A colleague and I went to see how we could get involved in supporting this work as a church, practically as well as financially. God spoke to me through the different situations and circumstances we came across. I saw more than twenty young people climb out of the hole in the ground that was their home. We met a young boy who had been living in one of the homes but longed to go back to living on the streets to beg for his survival. People I had met on my first visit who used to live on the streets were now living and working at the farm. God had started to develop their self-image, as they felt valued by the love that had been shown to them and by the opportunity given to them to work and develop new skills.

I met a girl of about 15 living in one of the homes and studying at school. Her face was a picture of joy as she showed me her work and her beautiful, neat writing. I felt so excited for her, and yet her friend of the same age had decided to stay on the streets and become a prostitute. You cannot help being affected by this, as you see the contrast of their young lives.

I would encourage every man reading this book to go and visit a mission, whether it be in this country or abroad, that is working with people like this. It will do you only good as you see how fortunate you are, but more importantly, God will once again break your heart emotionally and spiritually. You will become determined to make the most of every opportunity God gives you to serve him faithfully in all that you do.

I left that country humbled, broken and asking God to forgive me for my often selfish and ungrateful attitude. I wanted to be open to him to use me at any time in any way to bring hope to people. On the journey back to the UK, my mind was running a hundred miles per hour with the images we had seen and the stories we had heard. On our final flight to Manchester from Frankfurt, God challenged and encouraged me as he began to take me at my word. As the plane began to fill up, I said to God, 'If you want me to talk to anyone about you, I'm open for that.'

I was sitting nearest the aisle, when a gentleman came and asked if he could get to his window seat. No one else came and sat in our section, so we had three seats between the two of us. As the plane began to move down the runway, this man began to grab the side of his face and make some strange noises. At first I wondered if he was afraid of flying, but it became obvious that he was in some distress and pain.

He could not sit still. He kept pressing his handkerchief tightly against his left cheekbone while wincing and constantly moving his head into different positions. Once we were in the air he asked a steward for some painkillers as he had severe toothache.

It was then I felt God say to me, 'Why don't you pray for him?'

'Let's just see how the painkillers work, shall we?' was my reply.

But the man continued to do his armchair dance with sound effects! So, as the stewards came around with drinks, he asked them what painkillers they had given him, as they were not working. He was informed that they could only give out aspirins. A lady in front of us turned round and asked him if he would like some Nurofen, to which he quickly said yes. She told him she would get them out of her bag once the stewards' trolleys were out of the way.

I knew I had to ask him if he would like me to pray for him. It was either Jesus or Nurofen. I had to ask him before the trolleys moved further down the aisle. There was no way Nurofen was going to get the better of Jesus!

So I leaned over to this guy and said, 'Excuse me, sir, I'm a minister of a church.' I asked if he would like me to pray for him so that God would heal him.

He replied, 'Yes.'

So I prayed the following: 'God, you know the discomfort Peter is in. Will you please now come and heal him of all the pain so he can enjoy the rest of the flight, in Jesus' name? Amen.'

He echoed the 'Amen' quite loudly, and I turned round to see if anyone was looking! He grabbed my hand and thanked me. Minutes later he was taking the tablets.

I prayed in my mind and under my breath for about another twenty minutes, asking God to do something in this man's life. As the captain informed us of our descent to Manchester, Peter leaned over to me and said the pain had immediately started to go once I had prayed for him.

Life in the Spirit

I was introduced to the Holy Spirit about four years after I became a Christian. I now know that he came into my life on the day of my conversion, but no one explained that to me. When I was studying at a Methodist Bible college, every so often a visiting speaker would hold a 'Life in the Spirit' weekend. He or she would speak on the Saturday evening in the chapel to the student body and the staff, and again on the Sunday morning. This particular weekend the speaker spoke about being filled with the Holy Spirit.

I sat there listening to this man, wondering who he was talking about, until he explained what Jesus said about the Holy Spirit in John's gospel, chapters 14 and 16. As I sat and listened, I felt quite scared and unsure, as I had not heard teaching like this before. At the end of the meeting he offered to pray for anyone who wanted to be baptized or filled with the Holy Spirit. Quite a lot of students responded and went out for prayer. My four friends all went out to be prayed for and I quickly and quietly left the chapel and went to my room.

I had many questions racing through my mind as well as fears about what I heard and saw as people were being prayed for. Some of the students began to fall over, others just stood there looking quite peaceful and others started to speak in a different language, which I later found out was a new prayer language called speaking in tongues.

After the meeting had finished, my mates came to my room and started to discuss what had happened to them while they were being prayed for. As I listened to their different experiences, I started to feel angry that I had not been told earlier about the Holy Spirit and what he could and would do if we gave permission. My friends had all experienced different things, from a sense of a deep love, identity and peace to a greater awareness of who God was in their lives. Even though I knew I could do with all the above and more, I refused when they offered to pray for me. That night I did not do much sleeping but lots of questioning. Was this real or just hype? Was the Holy Spirit really the exact representation of Jesus? If I allowed him into my life fully, would it make a difference to my Christian life? Would I have to speak in tongues and sound as if I was saying, 'She came on a Honda', 'Keys for my Sierra' or 'Let's have a shandy'?

At the service the next morning, the last thing I wanted was to listen to that bloke again. When he got up to speak, I tried to switch off but couldn't. He began by explaining that he had intended to speak on a particular theme, but he believed God wanted him to speak again on the Holy Spirit. I don't remember anything about what he said; all I do remember is him saying, 'I believe there is one person who needs to come and see me afterwards in the vestry. I would like to pray for them and their fears about the Holy Spirit.' I knew he meant me, but how did he know?

I left the chapel as if I was going to my room as most of the students headed for the dining-room for lunch. When I thought the coast was clear, I headed for the vestry. I knocked on the door and entered. The gentleman was sitting there. I introduced myself, sat down and he began to ask me some questions. I had only been in there for what seemed five minutes when he asked if he could pray for me.

I didn't feel anything but was impressed with what he prayed. It was something like the following: 'God, you know this young man wants to serve and follow you the rest of his life. He knows he can't do this in his own strength and needs you to help him. Will you come now by your Spirit and fill him to overflowing with your love and peace? Take away all the fears he has of what might happen or what he should feel, and surprise him with the difference you will make in his life. Amen.'

I thanked him and went for my lunch, trusting God to answer his prayer. As I went on studying at college, I was aware of how God was changing me and helping me. The preacher's prayers were being answered.

Months later, after leaving college, I was working for a Christian friend of mine. Alan was a farmer and needed some help to do some potato-picking. I needed the money as I was unemployed, and I didn't mind doing it. The work consisted of me and two other fellows standing at the back of a trailer being pulled by the tractor. As the spuds were being dug up, they would come up a conveyor belt to where we stood. Our job was to sort the spuds from the soil so they could then go up another conveyor belt and be stored in the trailer being pulled alongside us.

Eight hours a day of this, and you soon get bored. After a few days I decided to take my personal stereo headset so I could listen to the radio or tapes to kill the boredom. One day I was listening and singing along to a tape of a Christian band, when out of the blue, this strange language started to come out of my mouth. The two guys I was working with began to look at me as if I had just landed from another planet. I certainly was singing as if I had!

What in the world was going on?

One minute everything was fine; the next, all chaos had broken out. I remember coming up with some explanation for the guys, which they bought. However, every time I tried to speak, there was this urge to speak in this different language. I could not wait for the day to finish so I could see my mate and ask him what was going on.

When I got to his house and he opened the door, I asked him, 'What's this?' I opened my mouth and out it came.

My mate smiled and said, 'That's tongues.'

'Why would God give it to me on the back of a tractor?' I asked. 'I thought it only happened when someone prayed for you at the end of a meeting.'

'God has given you this gift, so use it and don't abuse it. It is there to help you pray and worship, so just do that.'

This was the beginning of an awareness of who the Holy Spirit is and what his role is in the Christian life.

In 1995 a big cuddly man from California came over to Britain with a team to do numerous conferences around the country. His name was John Wimber, and it seemed people either loved him or hated him. I had never heard of this man but I went to the conference at the City Hall in Sheffield. It was all about Jesus using you by the leading of the Holy Spirit. It was tremendous to be in a packed hall with people worshipping God and to see the hunger there was from the delegates to hear about being more effective in sharing their faith.

During the first session John told his story – how God came into his life and dramatically changed his lifestyle. At the end of his talk, he encouraged us all to stand and said, 'God is here by his Spirit and wants to come and minister to each person in whatever way he chooses for you, to help you be more effective in the calling that's on your life.' As we stood, Wimber spoke those famous words which were to annoy many and bless thousands: 'Come, Holy Spirit.'

After a short while some people began to cry, shake, laugh or fall over, while others, like me, just stood staring at the things that were happening to them. I must admit I was feeling apprehensive and wondering if I was caught up in some clip from the film *The Blues Brothers!* Others stood silently with their eyes closed, looking quite peaceful. Wimber encouraged his team to begin moving among the people and start praying for them.

One of the Americans came up to me and said he believed that God had spoken to him about a situation in my life. He said God had shown him that when I was 15 I had been sexually interfered with. I could not believe what I was hearing! He was spot on, but I was not going to admit he was right, as I was embarrassed and angry with God that he would reveal such a thing.

So as casually as possible, and without blushing, I said to this guy, 'I'm sorry, but you're wrong.'

He graciously apologized and moved on to pray for others.

When I got home that night I sat for a while wondering how God had shown this man what had happened to me, and why?

The next day I was back at the conference hoping to hear from God, longing to be encouraged but also open to be challenged by him about areas of my life where sin ruled. When people were given the opportunity to receive prayer at the end of the meeting, I stood.

Then I noticed the guy from the previous night approaching me. *Please, God – don't do this to me!* I thought.

He smiled and immediately apologized, and then said: 'Last night I could not sleep as I believe God was speaking to me about you and what I shared with you last night. He told me that I had not made a mistake and it wasn't to embarrass you but because he wanted to heal you, so you would no longer be emotionally tied to that incident in your life.'

I looked at him with two thoughts running through my head, if that is possible for a man! They were *Go away!* and *Please let this be true!*

I stood there looking at him in silence, which seemed to last ages. Eventually I said to him, 'You are right – I'm sorry for lying to you yesterday.'

He just smiled and encouraged me to talk to a friend I could trust and let God begin the healing process.

How amazing God is! He sends over a guy from America who has never even been to this country before, never mind not knowing me, and speaks to him in such a way that God breaks into an area of my life that I had been carrying around for over ten years. I will always be grateful to God and to that guy for his holy obedience and for stepping out in faith.

That night I chose to tell my best mate Steve. As I sat in his lounge with his wife, Janice, I told him what had happened in the meeting. With a lot of fear I told them what had happened to me when I was 15 while I was having a trial for a football team. As I shared about the player coach sexually interfering with me, I waited for the look of disgust and the barrage of words coming back at me, saying how they did not want our friendship to continue. How wrong I was! Steve came over to me and hugged me, and slowly I began to cry until I could not control my emotions. I wept uncontrollably, with tears streaming down my face and snot running down my nose onto my mate's shirt, but he just kept hugging me. This was the beginning of God healing me of all the hurt, anger, hatred and pain that I had bottled up.

During the next few days at the conference I began to discover and experience more of God's love and power, as I heard stories of ordinary men and women being guided by the Holy Spirit to share their faith with people, pray for healing and even share words of knowledge and prophecy to people inside the church as well as outside. I remember saying to God in the final meeting of that conference, 'God, whatever you want to do in my life, do it, and I will try to be open and obedient to you so you can.'

Whenever anyone prays a prayer like that, I imagine God rubbing his hands together and saying to Jesus, the Holy Spirit and the angels, 'Now we are going to have some fun!' It was not long after this that I began to find God speaking to me in ways that I had not experienced before. Yes, he was still speaking to me through the Bible, when I prayed and when I went to church, but now he was speaking to me through pictures in my mind, thoughts and even pains in different parts of my body or heat in my hands. Sometimes I would be walking through the city centre and I would look at someone and then get a thought in my mind. It could be depression, hurt, sorrow or anger. I wish I could say that I always responded to these promptings from God, but I didn't.

Stepping out

Two occasions when I did step out created quite a stir. The first situation was on a Sunday morning. I had been asked the day before if I would play for a football team, as their goalkeeper was away – I was happy to oblige. The morning of the match, I woke up with quite a sharp pain in my back. I didn't know what was wrong, but it was sore. I played football that morning rather badly due to this constant pain.

After lunch I laid down on the settee as the pain increased. I was supposed to be speaking at a Methodist church in the evening. Eventually the pain was so severe that I decided to phone the church to explain that I would not be able to make the meeting that evening.

As I struggled to get to the phone, I felt as if the Holy Spirit was whispering to me, 'Don't cancel – go.'

I started to argue with God: 'Why should I go when I'm in so much pain?'

He replied, 'Because the pain you are in is what one of the members of the church has been suffering for years. Tonight I want to heal them.'

As I got ready for the service, I asked God what was wrong with the person. He replied that they had a trapped nerve in the spine.

I managed to drive to the church building and meet the people before the service started. As we began the service, the pain was getting more and more unbearable. I was pleased to get to the point where I was to speak. There were about fifty people in the church. I explained what had happened to me and what I believed God had said about someone having that pain for years, but tonight he wanted to heal them.

Straight away, a lady called Joan stood up and said, 'I'm healed. The pain has gone!' She started jumping and dancing around while we all looked on in amazement.

I thought, *Great! I carry this pain around all day and don't even get the opportunity to pray with her! I wonder why?*

The lady next to Joan saw what God had done and that night knew God was real. Within a week the whole street where Joan lived knew about her healing, including her husband, who responded, 'I know this is real because something has happened to you.'

I spoke to Joan while writing this chapter to make sure I had the facts right. Joan had been in constant pain for over five years with sciatica, and God began his healing in her life that night. What really surprised me when talking to Joan was that the pain did not fully leave her until Wednesday, and I still had the pain when I left the church, right up to Wednesday!

I wanted to be used more like this for God, so people's lives could be changed, whether they were Christians or not, and for Jesus to become more real in people's lives. The second occasion when I got a severe pain did not cause such a joyous reaction. I worked at the YMCA and organized a monthly meeting called 'Powerpoint' for teenagers from different churches in and around the city. The evening consisted of a Christian artist or band, plus a speaker who would challenge and encourage the teenagers to commit their lives to God and follow him. The evenings would attract anything from 200 to 600 teenagers, both Christians and those who didn't know Jesus yet.

One particular evening, my mate Steve was speaking and we had a group from York called Mimic, which included a mime artist and a soloist who played the guitar and keyboards. I remember the evening was a fancy dress night. During the day I started to get a severe pain in my left testicle while trying to play football. By the evening the pain had worsened and I was wondering if this was about someone who was going to be at the meeting.

I shared this with Steve and his response was, 'Well, I'm not sharing that – you can!'

I said to him, 'Let's pray that if this is God wanting to heal someone, then the pain will get worse.'

Afterwards I wasn't sure that was such a clever prayer! The evening began. Most people had arrived in fancy dress, as it was the Christmas special. The mime artist and soloist were excellent. Steve spoke well, and then we got to the response. By this time I was in serious discomfort. Steve had asked people to respond to whatever God had been saying to them. People became Christians, others were doing business with God about some area in their lives and others asked for prayer for healing in their lives. God was moving in that place and it was quite amusing to see people in fancy dress being prayed for.

Steve then came over to me and asked how the pain was. When I replied 'worse', he looked at me as if to say 'Great!' He then went back to the microphone and said, 'Baz would like to say something.'

My heart was pounding, my testicle aching, and I thought, *Please God, let this be you, and not me drawing attention to myself!* I wasn't sure how you talk about a left testicle in a Christian meeting. If it was a group of guys playing football and someone had the ball kicked in that region, we would know what to say, but I didn't want to offend anyone!

Well, eventually I began to speak and said, 'I believe tonight that God wants to heal a guy' – it certainly wasn't going to be a girl! – 'who has a problem with his left testicle.' As sensitively as possible, I encouraged this person to talk to a close friend after the meeting or in the next few days and get them to pray for their healing. I certainly was not going to ask them to come to the front for prayer and be embarrassed in front of the rest of the young people.

I was pleased I had shared what I believed God wanted me to, but nothing had prepared me for what happened next. A whole group of people got up and walked out of the building, obviously not happy with what I had shared. This caused me a lot of anxiety, as I knew these people and did not want to upset them or anyone else.

People continued to pray for one another. When everyone had gone and just a few of us were left to tidy up, I asked Steve to pray for me, as I was feeling very vulnerable since I had caused others to be upset.

Later, when all the equipment had been cleared away, I was in my office collecting a few things before I left for home. There was a knock on my door and a guy called James (not his real name) who worked at the YMCA asked if he could have a chat. He eventually informed me that he was the person with the left-testicle problem. It was twisted and he had a cyst on it and was due to go to the hospital on Monday to have it looked at. I asked him if he would like me to pray for him, to which he agreed. I asked God to finish what he had started and heal James of this problem. He left and I thanked God for encouraging me.

First thing on Monday morning, I had an assembly to do and then I went to the YMCA. Later on that morning, James came to see me to tell me how he had got on at the hospital. The cyst had gone and his testicle had gone back to the correct position – God had healed him!

I tell you these stories not to blow my own trumpet but, hopefully, to encourage you to step out for God when he speaks to you. The most important thing to remember is that God will not speak to you about a situation or person and ask you to do something about it and leave you by yourself. He will be with you. The Christian life is exciting and challenging, so why not let God take you on this adventure as he carries you along by his Spirit?

Questions

- What was your first experience of the Holy Spirit?
- What has been your most memorable experience of the Holy Spirit? Where was this? Why was this?

- When was the last time you gave yourself totally to the Holy Spirit? How did you feel? Did anything happen?
- In Ezekiel 47:1–12, we read about the river from the temple. How would you grade yourself today in connection with the picture that Ezekiel paints about the Holy Spirit? Are you: ankle deep; knee deep; waist deep; submerged; swimming with your feet and not able to touch the bottom?
- Have you any fears of the Holy Spirit?
- Have you had a bad experience in the past which is holding you back?
- Why do we need the Holy Spirit?
- Since the Holy Spirit is dwelling in the believer, isn't that enough?

I must be filled. It is absolutely necessary. I may be filled. God has made it blessedly possible. I want to be filled. It is eminently desirable. I will be filled. It is so blessedly certain.
Andrew Murray[47]

Logic is neither a science nor an art, but a dodge.

Benjamin Jowett (1817–93)

18

Adventurous Youth Work

Lee

There are loads of great things about being involved in youth work for years, as I have been. One is that some young people who you have worked with grow up and become your friends (and sometimes you even work with some of them too). But you also see fads come and go (remember the WWJD wristband and the Jabez prayer?). People, practices and techniques that were mainstream in my early years as a youth worker are no longer around now. For instance, on my Facebook page was a picture of me and Jimmy Savile.[48] Jimmy is a (slightly odd) legend here in Leeds, but the other day a 20-year-old said, 'Who's that man with you in that picture?' I was gutted – I thought everyone knew Jimmy! Now then, now then.

So as a veteran ex-youth worker, I want to make this controversial statement: 'I think we are letting down the lads we work with, by doing too much Bible study and worship!'

Let me explain. One of my youth-work heroes is Pip Wilson. He used to run 'The Rolling Magazine' tent at the Greenbelt festival in the 1980s, when I was 13. 'The Rolling Magazine' tent was the place to be – mad group games, loud music, a healthy sense of competition, snappy three-minute talks and famous guests. By the end of the two hours you were sweaty and tired, but you'd made new friends and left with a massive smile on your face (and if you were lucky, you had met the Radio 1 DJ Simon Mayo!). Pip is a legend,[49] but where are 'The Rolling

Magazine'-style youth groups and events these days? Where are the adventures, the physical games and a healthy sports slots, and even the snappy talks and life lessons? I went to one of those youth groups in Nottingham as a grumpy BMX-riding teenager, and it really helped keep me on my journey with God, even though I was a pain in the backside to the leaders most of the time.

I believe youth workers get paid (or volunteer) to be themselves. Whatever journey they are on, it is bound to spill over into their work. That is why they have to stay fresh (and not go off on random/dodgy tangents!). So as I have written two books helping lads and men, that has obviously affected my thinking, and I have started to ask questions similar to the ones that Dave Murrow poses in his book *Why Men Hate Going to Church*. Is the church (and therefore Christian youth work) becoming more feminine?

I wonder whether we have subtly changed our youth work into something it was never meant to be – a quiet house group that listens to quiet (folk-based) worship CDs and then does an hour's Bible study on abstract subjects such as the twelve Greek words for 'worship'.[50] By the way – asking questions like this doesn't make you an aggressive, oddly patriarchal male chauvinist, or even a sexist pig!

It's just a fundamental question to ask, like 'What is church?' Youth workers *must* ask big questions – it's their job.

Set up to fail?

The statistics say we are losing lads and men from the church. Maybe our youth-work style is a big, almost hidden factor in this decline. Maybe we are setting our young men up to fail.

Lads don't read as well as girls (they are usually two years behind), and because of the testosterone racing through their bodies, they don't sit still very well. But what do we often do?

We tell them to open a big book, read it out loud or sit still, quietly 'waiting on God'.

Ouch.

My friend Dave, a child psychologist, says, 'We must keep the lads in our youth work active. Mad games are great, especially for young to mid-teens.'

But does this mean we shouldn't teach the Bible?

Err, of course not, but we must find more creative and active ways to teach it, and that doesn't have to be done quietly!

That's one of the reasons why I am so in favour of 'community clean-ups', short-term practical mission and similar projects that get young people out there learning to serve God through action, not just words. We need to know that following Jesus is an active lifestyle, not a leisure-time club. It's more about getting our hands dirty with real people than candle-based meditation.

All I am saying is, lets get some balance.

If all our youth work is cerebral and abstract in nature, then let's have mad outdoor competitive times as well. If we always allow girls to win, we will lose our lads. Women can do masculine but men *don't do* feminine – that's a key to remember.

So, if we make our youth work more male-friendly, it is *not* off-putting to the girls we work with. It's a win-win.

And what about even going a stage further and incorporating male rites of passage into our youth work? Many other cultures have them, but we have defaulted our rites of passage here in the UK to having your first drink, fight or sexual experience. My friend Luke, a youth worker, did a rites-of-passage residential recently with a group of Christian (and not-yet-Christian) lads. He set outdoor challenges for them, and there was the chance that they might fail! We don't talk about failure very often, do we? But lads can learn so much from failure – it builds character and can even strengthen us. Kanye West mentions this in his song 'Stronger'. A fashion-obsessed 'bling-bling' man rapping about how failure has made him stronger – I didn't see that coming.

So, what if we stopped asking young men to be 'saved' and started challenging them to follow Jesus Christ? Oh yeah, and while we are asking big questions, 'Why do we think worship is just singing songs?' (as Shane Claiborne has asked).[51]

Suburban danger

Most churches I know are predominantly white and middle-class. Even those in urban areas are often filled by suburban people travelling in on a Sunday. I am convinced, like Shane, that one of the most dangerous places you can live is suburbia. If you want a man's faith to die, then make him safe/comfortable and watch him get bored and sometimes even depressed.

One of the greatest compliments I have ever received was from a young person who said to me and Clare, 'You are about the only married Christian parents I know who haven't gone safe and boring.' We were designed for adventure, as I was telling some young people recently. (I even went so far as to apologize for the church, which may have made their faith boring.)

We always try to make our lives safer and safer. I am guilty of that too. But safety means nothing without some risk or adventure.

God isn't tame, but he is good.[52]

And that should be reflected in our youth work and church life.

And lastly . . . Youth workers' training in recent years has often been more about health and safety than effective communication with young people. We need health and safety, just like we need auditors and accountants – but they don't make the values and flavour of our youth work. Fun and adventure aren't the first things that come into my mind when I think about auditors and accountants, but they should be when we think of youth workers!

Bring back the adventure – go easy on the candles.

Further reading/viewing

- *Why Men Hate Going to Church* by David Murrow
  (Thomas Nelson, 2006) www.churchformen.com
- *Boys Becoming Men* by Lowell Sheppard (Authentic, 2002)
  http://www.lowellsheppard.com/boys.htm

Only dull people are brilliant at breakfast.

Oscar Wilde (1854–1900)

19

Hide and Seek

Baz

Most people have come to prefer certain of life's experience and deny and reject others, unaware of the value of the hidden things that may come wrapped in plain and even ugly paper. In avoiding all pain and seeking comfort at all costs, we may be left without intimacy or compassion; in rejecting change and risk we often cheat ourselves of the quest; in denying our suffering we may never know our strength or our greatness.

Rachel Naomi Remen[53]

At the age of 17½ I became a Christian. Six months prior to that I was on the brink of death. I took a cocktail of alcohol and tablets. I did not want to die; it was just a cry for help and attention. While in hospital, after having my stomach pumped and numerous blood tests, I had three days of lying around thinking. Questions were rushing through my mind such as *What if I die? Where would I go? Is there a heaven or a hell?* I had no answers to these questions and neither did anyone else I knew.

I discharged myself from hospital and tried to get on with my life as if nothing had happened. Unfortunately, for the next six months, I went through a phase of depression. Up to that point, I thought depression was when the alarm went off in the morning. Now, if I was in a pub with my mates and somebody started laughing, I thought they were laughing at me. At work

I would be helping to put a central heating system in, when I would just start crying, not because I had flooded the house, but because something was going on deep inside my mind and heart. I refused to go and see the psychiatrist because of the fear of my mates finding out. I didn't want them to think I was going mad.

Six months later I went for a week's holiday with some of my friends who were involved with a youth club. The place we had gone to was Cliff College, which is based in the Peak District. Hundreds of other young people were there from all around the UK. This was an annual event called the Derwent Week. Most, if not all, of the young people were Christians. My friends and I decided that we would visit the local pub every night and get hammered. The main reasons for me being there were to get drunk and get off with a girl, but more importantly, to get away from home and escape from what was going on in my life.

Every morning I went along to one of the smaller meetings. I decided to go to one because I liked the look of a girl in the group from Bath. There were about thirty people in the group, all of a similar age. Each day we looked at some aspect of the Christian faith and the Bible, and each day the guy who was leading the group, Peter, would ask me for my opinion and I gave him a load of abuse about why I didn't believe in this stuff. I was trying really hard to upset and embarrass him. Every time he thanked me for my contribution and moved on, never looking flustered or shocked by what I had just said.

Ranting

I was there only because of this girl and because the pub wasn't open. However, God had me there for other reasons. Each day we went through the same process: Peter asking me to share, then me turning the air blue and him replying,

'Thanks for that, Baz.' Every time I started to rant, some of the group started to read their Bibles (yeah, right!) to hide their embarrassment about what was going on, but Peter just accepted me for who I was.

After five mornings together, Peter suggested that we made or bought a small present for the person we had been sitting next to all week. Yes, you guessed it – I had sat next to this girl. So I bought her a lovely white pocket-sized Bible and said something complimentary about her.

I had been sitting next to Peter and couldn't wait to see what he had bought me. Everyone else had given their presents to each other. I was the last one. Peter began by saying how much he had enjoyed the week, and how much he had appreciated my input. He went on to say, 'I've not bought Baz anything.'

I thought, *Great! I have spent pounds on that girl and he's not got me a thing. That's typical of a minister, the stingy beggar!*

He went on to say, 'I've written Baz a letter I want him to read later.'

A letter! I can't believe I'm hearing this! I thought.

He continued, 'I've also got him this.' He then pulled out of his pocket a rubber band. It was about six inches long and half an inch thick. I couldn't believe my eyes. He said that this represented my life at that moment, but if I let God into my life it could be 'like this' – he then stretched it to its full potential.

As he did this, something began to happen. I felt as if someone or something had punched me in the heart. I could feel all the anger and pain welling up inside. I wanted to shout, 'Will someone help me?'

I got up from my chair, grabbed the letter and the rubber band and ran out of the room.

When I was by myself, I opened the letter (which I still have today), and read:

Dear Baz,

It has been good to have you in the group this week. You have entered into everything very well, even when you were asked to share with me yesterday. I am going to comment on your enthusiasm when I say a word about you. I don't know if you have made that decision to give yourself to the Lord Jesus Christ. I can only encourage you to do so if you have not. The Christian life is the most demanding and costly life, but certainly the most joyful and satisfying. Trust that everything goes well for you in the immediate future and throughout your life.

Have a great day today.

Yours in his care,

Peter.

As I read the letter I knew that I had been kidding myself, thinking that my life was full when in fact it was desperately empty. The motivation of trying to be someone I wasn't was no longer helping. All day I kept thinking about Christianity and this guy called Jesus. Was it possible that I could know God for myself, like these young people said they knew him?

I arranged to see Peter before tea so I could talk to him privately about Christianity. He explained to me about the good news of Jesus: why he died on the cross, the consequences of sin and how I could know God's forgiveness and his love. I knew deep down this was what I wanted. I asked him what I needed to do, and he said simply, 'Pray.'

I had a problem with this. The only model I had seen was the vicar at the church I visited for Boys' Brigade services. He would whistle at the end of certain words or sentences. His voice also seemed to go up an octave when he prayed. Did I need to do that? Peter told me to talk to God as I would talk to my best friend. OK, I thought, here goes:

'God, my life is a bloody mess. I don't need to be told that I have sinned; I know I have. I have hurt a lot of people by what I've done and what I've said to them and about them. Will you please forgive me for this and other sins I have done? You know the anger, hatred and pain in my life – will you please deal with this? Thank you that your Son died for all the shit in my life; please forgive me and help me to be the person that you want me to be. God, will you please help this not to be a fad that lasts a few months, then fades away? Let this be for life. Will you please do something in my life so I that I can never say you don't exist?'

The voice

What I was asking him for was a miracle. I just sat there with my eyes tightly shut, waiting. After a few minutes' silence, Peter asked me, 'What are you waiting for?'

'The voice,' I replied.

'What voice?'

'The one you see and hear on those Moses films, where it sounds as if someone is talking into a bucket.'

He smiled and told me I didn't need to hear a voice; God had heard my prayer and had answered and would continue to answer.

And even though I didn't hear the voice, I felt a peace in and around me that I had never felt before. The news soon got around that the Northerner had found God. People were congratulating and hugging me, which I found a little strange. The following day many asked me how I felt. I still had this peace in my life, but also some doubts started to rise in my mind.

Some people informed me that they had seen a huge difference in me the next day, especially at meal times. The difference was in my language. I was no longer swearing when asking someone to pass the salt or water; I had moved from 'effing and jeffing' to polite requests.

Was this the miracle God was going to do? It certainly was. At school about fifteen of us had tried to stop swearing and had failed. God was showing me that all he wanted to do was to remove the rubbish from my life and replace it with something better. I will never speak Queen's English or be on *University Challenge*, and I cannot say that I have never sworn since that day, but I can say that it is no longer habitual in my life.

I need to explain the type of person I was before I became a Christian: one big Approval Addict. Even though I had started a new life, I still carried this huge area of rejection with me, which affected my motives at times. I was one of those people who had not just a chip on his shoulder but a whole chip shop!

The night I got home from this eventful week, I went straight back into the groove of things with my mates who had not been on the holiday. I was at a birthday party and we were drinking, dancing and having a good time, when all of a sudden I felt I was going to explode with excitement. I knew I had to tell everyone what had happened.

Be diplomatic, I thought, but I just let rip and shouted, 'I've met God!'

The response I got was amazing! Total silence. It was like someone had pressed the 'pause' button. The dancing, drinking and laughing stopped and the staring began.

'You've met *who*?' asked someone.

'I've met God,' I said.

Immediately there was uproar, from laughing to shouting obscenities.

Even though, from that day, I faced regular abuse or having the mickey taken, I was determined to still be there with my mates, showing that God was real and that he had changed my life and could do the same for them. I continued to go to the pubs and clubs, played football and rugby, and continued to be their friend. I wanted them to discover God too, but I felt quite isolated at times, especially at parties when they were getting drunk, sleeping around and fighting. Sometimes I felt I was missing out, even though I knew the opposite was true. My motivation for doing most things was my need to be affirmed and told 'well done'. What I needed was a good dose of God and his love. Robert McGee writes:

> Our self concept is determined not only by how we view ourselves but by how we think others perceive us. Basing our self worth on what we believe others think of us causes us to become addicted to their approval.
>
> We spend much of our time building relationships, striving to please people and win their respect. And yet, after all the sincere, conscientious effort, it takes only one unappreciative word from someone to ruin our sense of self worth. How quickly an insensitive word can destroy the self assurance we've worked so hard to achieve.[54]

In Romans we read:

> For you did not receive a spirit that makes you a slave again to fear, but you received the Spirit of sonship, and by him we cry '*Abba*, Father.' The Spirit himself testifies with our spirit that we are God's children. Now if we are children, then we are heirs – heirs of God and co-heirs with Christ, if indeed we share in his sufferings in order that we may also share in his glory.
>
> Romans 8:15–17

In *The Message* it reads:

> The resurrection life you received from God is not a timid, grave-tending life. It's adventurously expectant, greeting God with a child-like 'What's next Papa?' God's Spirit touches our spirits and confirms who we really are. We know who he is, and we know who we are: Father and children. And we know we are going to get what's

coming to us – an unbelievable inheritance! . . . If we go through hard times with him, then we're certainly going to go through the good times with him!

It is true to say that insecurities hinder our relationship with God and our development as a person. My best mate Steve has often said, 'People are secure in their insecurities.' People can be so afraid to trust God and move out of their insecurities into the security of God. It sometimes seems easier to stay in our comfort zones, even if they cause us a lot of pain, than to move into something new – the amazing love of God. If you have difficulty doing this, you will fall into the trap of seeking man's approval and you will eventually become an expert in the Approval Addict cycle. This will then determine what your motives are. I regularly fall into this trap and I'm so grateful for my wife Linda and my close friends who tell me when I do so.

Professionals and amateurs

As men of God we need to develop our intimacy with God and let him get closer to us. I was once at a church meeting where the speaker was talking about how the church has created an environment of two groups of Christians: the professionals and the amateurs. This caused the majority of people to feel that they needed to be seen to be doing something at the front to be really accepted by God and the rest of the church. Again, this would reinforce the need to be approved for all those who struggle in this area.

The speaker went on to say that even though it has never been taught publicly from the front of most churches, the actions of the leaders speak for themselves. He produced a roll of the tape that the police use when there has been an accident or a crime has been committed, to put around the scene of the incident to warn people that this is a restricted area. The words

'No unauthorized personnel beyond this point' were revealed as he and his wife unrolled the tape across the front of the church. He continued to explain that this is what the church and its leaders have done for centuries, not always by their words but often by their actions.

This rang true with me as I recalled some of the conversations others had had with me recently about what they were or weren't allowed to do. The speaker continued that many people feel like second-rate Christians, not authorized to do anything, due to a lack of encouragement or not being allowed to go beyond a certain point. He said that many felt that if they didn't get the opportunity to do something at the front of church they would never be fulfilled. He implied that this was a lie that would hold people back from achieving all that God had for them. He insisted that it is not about being seen up front but about being released and given permission to succeed with whatever God wants you to be involved with in the real place of need: the world.

As he and his wife held the tape at chest height, he encouraged those who related to what he had been speaking about to run through the tape and rip it up. He counted to three and nearly everyone ran to the front. Shouting, crying, stamping on the tape, people were doing business with God and allowing him to bring his freedom and healing to their lives. I was up there, ripping the tape, asking God to help me with the areas of my life where I fell into the trap of seeking man's approval. God did something powerful that day. I know the desire began in me to release the people of God into whatever God has for them and not hold them back. I have often failed, but it is still my passion.

I love the following quote by Martin Scott: 'Don't let the past dictate your future, but let the future dictate your present.' This can only happen when we put ourselves into a place where God is given permission to deal with the past. Most men are very good at keeping busy but not very good at sitting still.

We need to 'Be still, and know that I am God' (Ps. 46:10). As we do this, God can instil in us a holy confidence and security, which will help us to have purer motives in the things we do for him.

Is this what Jesus was trying to do when the seventy-two disciples returned excited about what had been happening? They returned with joy and said, 'Lord, even the demons submit to us in your name' (Luke 10:17).

Jesus replied, 'I saw Satan fall like lightning from heaven. I have given you authority to trample on snakes and scorpions and to overcome all the power of the enemy; nothing will harm you. However, do not rejoice that the spirits submit to you, but rejoice that your names are written in heaven.'

I love being used by God, whether it's sharing my story with people, working in schools, preaching, praying for people for healing, listening to people, prophesying, encouraging and releasing people, or giving people words of knowledge, especially in places outside the church setting such as pubs and restaurants. Whatever opportunity he gives me, I love to do it. However, I have often acted like the disciples and returned home, blowing my own trumpet. Why? Because like most men, I am insecure.

Get a group of men together and listen to their conversation and you will soon be able to determine if they are secure in God or not. Quite often it ends up like the song: 'Anything you can do, I can do better.' 'No, you can't.' 'Yes, I can.' We try to outdo one another with the best story!

Oh God, please help us. If we need any motivation to live and work for God, let it be because of what he has done for us. We have been given a new life, a brand new start – let's live as if we believe it. Let us be good news to others.

'You did not choose me, but I chose you and appointed you to go and bear fruit – fruit that will last' (John 15:16). This is what God says to all the men in the church. How fruitful are you?

One of the best motivators ever is the fact that you woke up this morning, still breathing! This means God still believes you can be useful for him. You have been given another chance to make a difference in this world and to someone else's life. Surely that must make you feel special! George New and David Cormack write:

> Motivation is an ever present influence in every sphere of your life. Your motives determine your enthusiasm and your satisfaction in every situation, whatever you are doing and wherever you are – at home, at work, with friends and even when you are alone. Motives are your constant companions. They have been with you since childhood. It is about time you became more acquainted![55]

Questions

Please work through these questions, preferably with someone you know and trust.

- What motivates you right now with your walk with God?
- Have you recognized any areas of your life where you fall into being an 'Approval Addict'? Is there a regular pattern to this occurring?
- How do you feel when you are with a group of men: secure or intimidated?
- Do you feel your life is fruitful for God? If not, what changes do you need to make? What changes do you need to allow God to make?
- Do you find it easy to be still in God's presence?
- Are you 'good news' to be with?
- Does your past dictate your future, or does your future dictate your present?

I like your Christ, I do not like your Christians. Your Christians are so unlike your Christ.

Mohandas Gandhi (1869–1948)

20

Why I Hate Religion

Baz

When I was younger I was a very angry young man. Nowadays there are only a few things that really get me angry: the injustice in the world; footballers complaining that they do not get paid enough whilst diving around like ballet dancers; politicians who tell us how we should live our lives and then do the opposite; and the way the church so often kills the life in people by its religious behaviour.

What do I mean by this? Well, whether it is a denominational church or a Christian fellowship, it is so easy to become religious in what we do and why we do it. Anything which takes the life out of our relationship with Jesus is religion to me. Religion kills.

A friend of mine who leads a church for men in America, recently said the following: 'They looked good on the outside but on the inside they were dead.'[56] Good on the outside but dead on the inside – this is what religion does.

As you may know, that is why I am on a mission to ban the word 'fine' in church. I hate it when you ask someone, 'Hi, how are you today?' and they say 'Fine', when really they are not fine but probably screwed up with anxieties, financial worries, depression, hurt or even suicidal thoughts. Outwardly they are trying to look good when inside they are bad.

Why do people say 'Fine'? Is it because they suspect that the person who is asking how they are doing probably does not want to know what is really going on in their lives but is just doing the religious thing? Or is it because they feel that as a Christian they can't be anything but OK?

I was helping out on an Alpha course some time ago and we had a gentleman named James (not his real name) attending. Every week I would say hello to him and ask him how he was doing, and he would always reply, 'Fine, thanks, Baz.' Unfortunately, James committed suicide about six months later. Obviously he was not fine but felt he could not share what was really going on in his life.

Someone has said 'FINE' stands for 'Feelings Inside Never Expressed'. Why does this happen? Because we have created a culture in church where we don't really want mess but we want to look nice. Well, let me tell you, 'nice' does not change anything, but it does chain people up and stop them from being real, relevant and transparent, and discovering the fullness of life that Jesus offers.

I hate religion. I hate the games people play in church and the way the church has stopped people from being themselves.

Philip Yancey says, 'There is nothing you can do to make God love you more and there is nothing you can do to make God love you less.'[57] What a powerful statement, if we could only get hold of it.

Why else do I hate religion? Because it creates a drivenness in Christians to perform, to try to win God's and others' approval rather than just being themselves.

All God is asking of me is to be the best Baz I can be: nothing more and nothing less. This is the same for you. This is easy to say but hard to practise, as we are all affected by what we think others think of us.

Questions

Ask yourself:

- Do you worry more about the outside than the inside?
- Are you honest about what's going on?
- Do you allow others to be honest?
- Do you want raw and real or 'nice'?
- Have you become religious and trapped rather than a free Christian?

As long as you live, keep learning how to live.

Seneca (Roman philosopher, first century AD)

21

Sorry to Bother You . . .

Lee

This chapter speaks for itself, and many people have spoken to me about the story below about my wedding night! The curse of niceness breeds dualism, the enemy of reality. More reality = less burn-out.

What's the slowest thing on four legs?
Two Christians trying to get through a door!
Tim Vine, comedian

What's this? – 'Oo, sorry . . .''Oo, sorry . . .''Oo, my mistake . . .'
'Oo sorry . . .''Oo . . . please forgive me.' – The bumper cars at a
Christian conference.
Tim Vine

What the world needs is people who are alive.
Gil Bailie[58]

It seems that most British people think we should be polite the whole time, and so a British person who is also a Christian is probably the politest and the 'nicest' person you've ever met – certainly in public, anyway. This cultural absurdity was brought to light in the TV programme *The Human Zoo*, where a group of people were asked to stay in a room until someone came to collect them. A fake fire was set off in the next room, and smoke poured in. The smoke alarm went off, but no one moved. They were just too polite and too embarrassed to do anything about it, and the fire officers in attendance said that if the fire had been real, they would have been dead within four minutes!

Bulldog spirit

When I met Ivan and Isobel Allum from Toronto, they gave me a ten-minute prophecy that said I was to be a 'brawler' in the kingdom of God. The prophecy didn't say I was to be 'a nice, lovely man of God', but a fighter – a man of violence in the kingdom of God.[59]

Another prophecy I received was that someone saw me as a British bulldog! He didn't know I was English at the time. I thought to myself, *That's not very polite – surely he means I'm a nice man of God!* But no – he said, 'You are a British bulldog, and you are standing in front of young people and you're protecting them from the enemy.'

So immediately after that I did some research on bulldogs and also have a picture of a bulldog for my desk at home. The original dogs were not like the ones we see now, with breathing and skin problems because of over-breeding, but they were used as fighting dogs and for bull-baiting. Their jaws were strong enough to grab a bull by its nose and hold it still while the farmer did whatever he had to do. And once the dog had hold, he wouldn't let go, even to the point of death. Bulldogs were full of tenacity and didn't give up.

Over the last few years, I've had some funny stares and fingers pointed at me when I've been in meetings and conferences, not only because of the occasional strange haircut, but because I often take a drum to worship God and to pray over people. I would pound this Dolak (an Indian drum) as hard as I could, and put the drumstick onto people's stomachs when I prayed for them. It isn't a polite or nice thing to do, but something I felt was needed.

Also, as mentioned previously, I occasionally carry round a replica (metal, not plastic) of the sword which Mel Gibson used in the film *Braveheart*. This doesn't fit with English reserve or with a traditional view of Christian men, but it's been an enormous help to me to rely on these weapons of war in the real fight that I'm here for in Leeds.

I have some great friends who have really got a 'warrior spirit' too. Baz is an example of that, as well as many others, who literally fight their way to God. They push through and are not afraid to make mistakes – and believe me, we have all made quite a few.

The Bible is a radical book, but we've managed to make it 'nice' and sterile over the years.[60] A classic example of this is the Good Samaritan in Luke 10. There have been many different versions of this, and I remember in the eighties the drama of 'The Good Punk Rocker', where the Samaritan would be a punk or a biker. But I still didn't realize the stigma that was attached to Samaritans, as hated people who were not part of the Jewish race. The thought that a Samaritan could help someone would be completely offensive to the people of Jesus' time.[61]

A similarity can be drawn to the woman at the well in John 4. Not only was she a Samaritan, but she was also a woman, and possibly a woman of 'dubious character'. Jesus was being radical to even talk to this person, let alone meet her and ask her for a drink. But somehow, over the years, we have made these things appear sterile; we've made them polite and nice.

And as John Eldredge says in his book *Wild at Heart*, we've made the pinnacle of Christian manhood becoming a 'nice guy'. 'Nice' is probably one of the most over-used and, to me, offensive words in the dictionary. It removes the chance of finding a true identity from people – especially men.

Don't take the path of humility because you are trying to be nice or to please people. Don't walk in simpering weakness. Choose to lay down your strength and serve.
John Eldredge[62]

I have a reputation among my friends for speaking my mind. I try to do it as appropriately as I can (although I have been known to fail!), but just occasionally I want to speak my full mind rather than keep things to myself. And this continues into all areas of my life, including shopping. I believe that if we're not happy with products, or if they're faulty, then we should complain. Let's take them back to the shop. Do it in the right, balanced way, but actually get what we paid for. It seems that a lot of Christians just don't complain, because they would rather be 'nice'.

I remember on our wedding night, my wife and I had a room at Manchester Airport's hotel before we were due to fly to New York the next day. As you can imagine, this night was something I had looked forward to ... for the whole of my life! We were given our room number and travelled what seemed like a mile down endless characterless corridors to find our room. We got there and I picked up Clare to carry her across the threshold. When we opened the door, we saw, to our horror, what every bride and groom would not expect to see – two single beds! So without a pause I said to Clare, 'Right, you wait there!' I ran to the reception area and told them in no uncertain terms that I was about to exercise my new marital freedom and I could not do that in a single bed! They obviously saw the severity of the situation and rectified it immediately. That story stops here, lads.

The best way to avoid becoming a constant moaner, of course, is to tell people when you are happy as well. I thanked a waitress once for her excellent service, and she didn't know what to do – it was hilarious!

Humble pie

Recently on different projects, I've been involved in the whole fundraising process by writing to trusts, businesses and local churches to secure our future through raising money. One of the first things I realized as I started this was that I must get rid of false humility: 'Oh, they won't give us any money; surely we're not worth it; we're only a little project . . .' But actually, when you're fundraising you have to say that you are doing a good job, and you are worth the contribution you're requesting.

In my travels with my band HOG, I spent a lot of time with gifted musicians, and for a while it wasn't very fashionable to take on the praise that people gave you. The correct answer would be, 'Give the glory to the Lord, not me . . .'

Now, when someone says I'm a good DJ, I do give glory to God because he gave me the gift, but I also say, 'Thanks a lot', because it makes me feel good to know I am a pretty good DJ! I'm not the best, and I'm not going to show off about it, but I welcome encouragement. That's very different from just pointing to the sky and whispering, 'It's just the Lord's glory.'

If you're a good guitarist, or a good businessman, then let people say it, and let's take on real compliments, to make the world slightly more realistic – especially in the church. Of course, if you don't hold your tongue all the time, it may appear that you are slightly rude. Often, it's not rudeness, just boldness in telling the truth.

I wonder how many church members have got more garden equipment than they need or can afford, simply because they're too embarrassed to ask to borrow it? If we need a lawnmower, I'll ask my neighbour and he'll lend me one; then we'll lend him our hedge-trimmers. And actually in churches and neighbour-hoods, that is how we need to be. In doing this we see more of each other and become more of a community. It's just that we need to have the guts to say, 'I need this. Can you help me?'

> *Most English people's goal in life is to get to the grave without ever being embarrassed.*
> John Cleese[63]

This is particularly relevant in fundraising, where as a youth-work organization we needed lots of equipment, computers, video projectors and so on. I've found that being very specific with people is helpful. So writing to organizations and saying, 'I need this from you; can you give it to me?' is much more helpful than, 'Please can you help me?' Let's not be over-polite, and maybe we can get the things that we need to do our work more effectively.

I spent my teenage years cringing at Christian events because of the various T-shirts that were around. Thankfully, there are some great (and still some not-so-great) Christian T-shirt manufacturers and designs now, but when I was growing up it was literally pictures of cute turtles and butterflies with comments which implied, 'Jesus is very nice indeed.' For a teenage lad growing up, those T-shirts and sweatshirts couldn't have been any further from the person that I was and the tastes that I had as a DJ. I was trying to find a voice in the Christian world to express the gifts that I had, and cute turtles had nothing to do with it.

God isn't 'nice' to us. He loves us and he likes us, but he's not a 'nice' person, because a 'nice' person wouldn't actually discipline us, wouldn't actually make us fit to run the race. The grace of God is not being nice. The grace of God is undeserved favour. If God were just nice, he wouldn't give us the Holy Spirit to prod us and change our attitudes, to push us in deeper with him, and to convict us of sin. I'm just thankful that God loves me and likes me, but is willing to challenge me.

The following story, taken from the Assemblies of God archives, is from Smith Wigglesworth's account of a visit he made to Belfast in 1926:

One day at 11 o'clock I saw a woman with a tumour. She could live out one day. I said, 'Do you want to live?' She could not speak. She just moved her finger . . . I said, 'In the name of Jesus,' and I poured on the oil. The doctor said, 'She's gone.' A little blind girl led me to the bedside. Compassion broke me up for the child's sake . . . carrying the mother across the room I put her up against the wardrobe. I held her there. I said, 'In the name of Jesus death come out!' Like a fallen tree, leaf after leaf, her body began moving – upright instead of lifeless. Her feet touched the floor. 'In Jesus' name walk!' I said, and she did, back to bed. There was a doctor there, sceptical. He saw her. She said, 'I was in heaven, countless numbers, all like Jesus. He pointed and I knew I had to go.'

Smith grabbed this dead woman, pushed her against the wardrobe and shouted at her to live! That wasn't very polite, was it? But it worked.

Questions

- What makes you most embarrassed?
- Read and discuss Luke 19. How would you have reacted to this situation?
- What is false humility?
- What makes you hold back from saying what you think?
- What does the fear of people look like in daily life?

*I am extraordinarily patient,
provided I get my own way in the end.*

Attributed to Margaret Thatcher

22

Over Ten Years to Walk 350 Miles

Baz

Over ten years ago I was with a group of people who travelled down to Southampton from Sheffield to see Delirious? at a gig in the Southampton Community Church building. During the event I had a strange thought that I should walk from Sunderland to Southampton, but quickly dismissed it as caffeine wearing off. As the evening went on, the thoughts kept returning: surely God was not asking this of a guy who hates walking if you can drive there!

The concert was over and we headed back up north to Sheffield, and I had quickly pushed the thought aside. However, God did not give up so easily and very patiently kept reminding me every so often over the next ten years about what he had asked me to do.

So on Monday, 5 June 2006, I stood outside a small church hall in Monkwearmouth, Sunderland, ready to start the walk. 'Why there?' you ask. Well, as I had prayed and looked into why God was asking me to do this walk, I felt it was to do with Smith Wigglesworth's prophecy from 1947 about the Word and the Spirit.[64]

This little church hall I stood outside was where Smith Wigglesworh had been baptized in the Holy Spirit. The church I was headed for in Southampton, Above Bar Church, has a good reputation as a Word church. It is also very connected to the Keswick convention, which was the other place where Wigglesworth was impacted hugely by the Holy Spirit. This walk was all about asking God to bring this prophecy into fulfilment in our nation and letting people see what our loving Father is all about. Instead of looking for the feel-good factor from a group of eleven over-paid men kicking a bag of wind around in Germany, thinking this will change the state of our nation, I wanted to play some small part in praying for the fulfilment of the prophecy.

As I stood outside the church hall praying, wondering if I would ever make Southampton, my phone rang: Steve Lowton was on the line to encourage me and pray for me. How good is our Dad? It was great to hear a friendly voice and to be prayed for by someone who knew exactly all the emotions I was feeling, as he has walked the length and breadth of our nation, also through Europe and the whole west side of America.

As I began walking, all I could think was how hard this could really be. I was to find out in the next two weeks. My feet blistered and bled most days, and I did a great impression of Poirot and how he walked, as I averaged about fifteen miles a day.

Through the pain, tears and feeling sorry for myself, I managed to get into a rhythm. As the feet healed up, I felt stronger and enjoyed the pilgrimage I was on.

I was very surprised by the response from people I talked to along the route. I received comments like 'Thank you for doing this – our country needs prayer' and 'This is great – well done!' and similar encouragements, all from people who wouldn't profess to be Christians. I even had a taxi driver pay for the cost of my taxi fare when he took me back to pick my car up, as he thought what I was doing was good. I had the opportunity to pray for a lady at a bus stop who was dying of cancer.

During my walk I stopped outside every school and church, asking God to bless and move in these places. As I entered one city, I felt God say to me that I needed to contact the Mayor and inform him that two councillors were stealing money – which I have done.

During my walk I felt some days that I really connected with heaven and had a good day of praying. Other days, it felt like I connected with God for about two minutes, and then the heavens were closed. At those times I remembered what my friend Steve Lowton said: 'Remember, Baz – your walk is your prayer. Anything else is a bonus.'

On Wednesday, 26 July 2006 I entered Southampton, relieved, excited and feeling quite surprised that I had managed to complete this walk. But as I sat outside Above Bar Church and prayed, it did feel quite an anticlimax. I went inside, asking God to continue to bless this church. Fifteen minutes later I was inside Community Church praying for Billy and Caroline Kennedy and the people of their church, excited that I was finishing off the walk in the same place where God had spoken to me about doing it over ten years earlier.

So, 24 days during a period of 7 weeks to walk 350 miles to accomplish what God had asked of me. What have I learnt through this? Whatever God asks of us, he will help us to do, as we try to be obedient to his requests.

I am so grateful for the love and support of Linda my wife, and for the prayers and encouragement from all the great folk at my church, the Eccles – especially the eight members who joined me on parts of the walk. Thanks too to my friends around the country for their emails and texts.

Has God asked you to do something, and you are still wondering how, why and when? Let me encourage you to talk to some of your mates and together to pray that God will give you all you need to step out, trusting that he will help you accomplish what he has asked of you. It is worth the excitement, pain, fulfilment and joy you will experience and the great lessons you will learn.

Some of my best leading men have been dogs and horses.

Attributed to Elizabeth Taylor

23

The Fun Factory!

Andy

This has always been my favourite chapter from Dead Men Walking, *not only because Andy is a mate and I know this story is true, but also because it is a great example of God working in a situation that seemed almost hopeless. I was so taken by this story that I got Andy to garble it into a dictaphone so I could make a chapter out if it to share with you lot. Cheers, Andy . . .*

It all happened around 1990 when I got a position in a church in the north-east of England. The church couldn't afford to pay any of my wages or expenses, so I had to get a job, and at the time the unemployment rate was terrible. It even got to the stage where I asked the local window cleaner if he wanted a lad to carry his ladders.

I was so distressed that I went to see my regional superintendent (a church boss person), and he went through all the patronizing patter about 'Have you tried to find a job? Where have you tried?' and so on.

I told him the full extent of my efforts to try and get employment, and his eyes lit up when I mentioned the window cleaner. This was the last resort for me, but he said, 'You get yourself a window cleaning round and I'll buy your ladders for you!' What an encouragement!

Lisa and I were planning to get married at the time. I just cried my eyes out and said to her, 'If this is what the ministry is all about, don't get married to me – go and find somebody who can look after you.' I was really fed up.

But I decided that if that's what God wanted me to do, then I would do it. Lo and behold, when I went back up to the north-east the following week, there was a letter through my door which said that I had an interview at a factory making lanse pipes for the steelworks. (These are massive ceramic pipes through which oxygen is blown.) I went for the interview and got the job. It was filthy work, and I used to come home every day looking like a coalman, covered in dust and grime and other terrible stuff.

Sores

After a while at work I started coming out in incredible sores all the way up my arms and back, all across my torso, and down my legs. I went to the doctor to try and get this sorted out, and he sent me for tests. The tests at the hospital involved drawing a big grid on my back of about forty-eight little squares and putting a different type of stuff on each square, to see if I was particularly allergic to anything. I had to keep this on for a week. I couldn't shower, as it was stuck on by sticking plaster. It was very uncomfortable, and because I worked in such a filthy job, not being able to shower was a nightmare. After a week, the only thing I was allergic to was the sticking plaster that they stuck the test on with!

The doctors eventually found out through my pinching stuff from work that some of the material we were working with was radioactive, and the boss had never told us! The boss never found out that it was me who had taken the stuff, but he was forced to sort out his working practices, which was well overdue.

The lads who I worked with were typical north-easterners, plus one lad from Norwich. As time went on the lads did seem to like me, but when they found out I was a Christian and training for the ministry – well, that was it. I was the butt of every joke and they tried every little thing to make me swear or look at a pornographic picture – that was their mission.

I had to hide my sandwich-box or it became a target. It started off with nuts and bolts in my sandwiches. Then it got steadily worse. Once I found a dead mouse in my lunch-box, and then they started peeing in my sandwiches – it just got foul. I thought if I laughed along with it they would pack it in eventually. I used to have to carry my tea mug around with me everywhere because they frequently peed in it and worse. This was pretty disgusting, I must admit, but it wasn't harming me in any way – it was their perverse way of having fun.

I drove around in my car for three weeks with a number-plate on the back that they had made – with the letters W-A-N-K-E-R. I wondered why I would get strange looks at traffic lights. I parked it outside church for three weeks and no one even noticed! At least, they'd not said anything to me.

Then it started getting serious. I found my car tyres slashed a couple of times. I also found that they had tried to sabotage my job in the factory. The boss who owned and ran the factory said I was the only person he could trust to determine what levels of raw materials went into each mixture, because over the years each lad who'd had a grievance against the company had deliberately sabotaged the mixture. He was a Shinto Buddhist, and even though he mocked me for being a Christian, he told me that I was the only person he could trust. I then found out that the lads were deliberately not measuring their particular end of the raw materials to try and get me sacked. That really did annoy me.

Then it got even worse and they started to try to physically harm me. The overhead crane, for obvious safety reasons, could only be taken up the factory if the hook was well above head height. One day I was working on the floor of the factory, bolting a mould together, with my back to the crane hook which was coming up the factory. The noise of the crane never used to bother me at all because you just got so used to it. I didn't realize that the person who was operating the hook had deliberately lined it up to hit me as it came up the factory. It got me square in the back, knocked the wind out of me completely, and sent me flying. I must say, it was a struggle not to cry – it was such a massive metal hook.

Every night I used to go home and pray, 'Lord, just help me get through this next day and help me show these lads what being a Christian is really all about.'

I used to have a sense of humour about things. For instance, the toilet cubicles were full of pornographic magazines – I used to pick all the porn mags out of one cubicle, pile them in the other toilet and make a big sign for the door saying, 'porn-free bog'. I just thought it was a good way of showing my faith without being too prudish. That didn't work, because they still ended up coming back into the toilet that I used, and so I then started shredding up their favourite pictures and flushing them away. When they found out, I must admit that didn't go down at all well. But I enjoyed it!

A mean streak

It got to the stage where I could take it off most of the lads in the factory, but there was one character who wound everybody up. He was the lad who was from Norwich. Nobody particularly liked him; he had a real mean streak in him. He was a bit of a head case and really had it in for me. He always took it that one stage further . . .

Every month the factory would stop production for a morning and we would clean up. This meant cleaning out the moulds, the mixers, the floor and generally making it tidy and safe. My job (because I was small) was to get inside the mixer (which was like an enormous cement mixer) and chip all the old mixture off the blades with a pneumatic drill. Obviously this meant turning the power off on the mixer to make it completely safe.

I remember drilling away one day and just stopping my drill for a minute to get rid of some of the old mix. Even though my ears were ringing from this drill, I heard the very distinctive buzz of the transformer starting on the mixer. This could only mean one thing – that the power had been turned on. I knew I had to get out of that mixer as quickly as possible or I would be killed – the blades would start spinning and that would be the end of me!

I had a matter of seconds to get out, so I leapt to my feet, chucked the drill out of the top hatch and climbed up onto one of the blade arms. Just as I pushed out the top hatch, the blade that my leg was on just started to spin round. I just made it out.

This nutter from Norfolk had deliberately switched on the power and, whether he meant to or not, could have quite easily killed me. That really did affect me. I could put up with all the messing about, the jokes and the taunting – but that was complete lunacy!

Later that month I'd had a particularly bad week. I'd already turned my car over on the way to work and ended up in a river! One lunchtime we were playing cricket – we'd made this big heavy cricket bat out of some pallet planks. I was batting, the lad from Norfolk was the backstop and somebody else was bowling. The Norfolk lad had been on at me all day long. I can remember him saying something that was particularly offensive. I can't even remember what it was now – probably something directed at either my mum or my girlfriend. And I just flipped.

I turned round with this cricket bat and hit him as hard as I could on the side of his legs. He went down like a felled tree, but I then continued to hit him with the bat. I didn't whack him round the head, but I just kept whacking him.

After about the fifth hit, the voice inside my head said, 'What on earth are you doing?'

All the lads were shouting, 'Go on, kill him!' They were really loving it, as they didn't particularly like him either.

But this voice said, 'You are going to lose your job, you're going to jail and this bloke is going to sue you for damages.'

I just stopped and burst out crying. Throwing the bat down, I said to him, 'I am really, really, really sorry.'

This lad, who was ten inches taller and about four stone heavier than me, just looked at me with frightened eyes and said, 'That's all right, I deserved it.'

Anyway, I got a good talking to by the boss and was told to go home early. I went home and cried my eyes out. I felt I'd completely blown my witness and put them off Jesus for ever. I said sorry to God for all that I'd done. The next day I went to work very sheepishly, not really anticipating what the lads would do or whether I'd even have a job.

But the lads were completely different to me! They didn't even wind me up. (They were probably scared that I was going to hit them with a cricket bat!) They had actually seen a human side to me and, one by one, they approached me and they talked about genuine prayer requests they had. One was in trouble with his marriage, another one's mum was ill with cancer, and another one had a disabled brother. They were asking me to pray for them. It was unbelievable – I really thought I'd blown my witness, and yet this was the breakthrough!

They had probably seen me as Super-Christian, able to withstand all this pressure and persecution. But as soon as I showed a bit of my human side, they warmed to me and they started to respond to my faith. It was a brilliant opportunity.

From that point on, I was one of the boys and they genuinely respected me, which felt very odd! Soon after this, the YTS boy had his finger chopped off in one of the machines.

Exorcism

The Shinto Buddhist manager, who was very superstitious, turned to me and said, 'Andrew, are you an exorcist?'

I looked very puzzled and said, 'You what, Mr Kato?'

He said, 'You get rid of demons, yes?'

I said, 'Well, if anybody asks me to – yes, I suppose I do!'

He said, 'OK, next Wednesday, we will shut down the whole factory and you will bring your Bible and you will pray and you will get rid of the evil spirit that cut Ken's finger off and tried to kill you. Then we will have a big barbecue with lots of alcohol.'

All the lads cheered!

I sort of said, 'Well, yes, OK, Mr Kato.'

The following Wednesday the boss got all the workers out of the factory – about thirty-five in all. They stood in the car park getting the barbecue ready, and I was able to go round the whole factory, praying for each individual worker. I didn't cast any evil spirit out of the place or anything like that, but I did pray for each individual. I prayed for safety – it was such a dangerous place, with accidents happening all the time. I prayed for a lot more unity and love about the place, as everybody was stabbing each other in the back and sniping about each other.

When I had finished praying, I opened the big double doors which led out into the car park, feeling like John Wayne coming out of a gun-fight!

As I went out, people came to me and said, 'Did you see anything? Did anything confront you?' I had a chuckle to myself and said, 'Some things are best not talked about.' I really loved it!

Then Mr Kato came over and gave me a cheque – I liked getting paid to pray! It was a fantastic opportunity, and from that day until I left, six months later, there wasn't a single accident in the whole of the factory.

The atmosphere in the factory among the workers improved as well. Mr Kato used to stand at the side of the clocking-in machine to say goodbye to everybody, and then he would to say to me, 'Ah, Andrew – no accidents this week.'

'Yes, Mr Kato – that's God!'

What a fantastic God we have! I thought I'd blown it, but you only need to be open to God, accept his forgiveness when you make mistakes, and just get on with things. God really does help you.

Questions

- How do you feel when people mock you?
- How do you hide the 'real you' from other people?
- Does it make them respect you more when you show your vulnerability?
- What stories do you have from work?

People go from denial to despair and miss the bit in the middle.

Al Gore[65]

24

Zany Gob Case

Baz

He who asks is a fool for five minutes,
but he who does not ask remains a fool forever.
Chinese proverb[66]

Have you ever been encouraged by your friends to do something which you later regretted? This was always happening to me when I was a teenager and, unfortunately, I would never back down. We would dare each other regularly, hoping that someone would fail or be caught. A dare back home was called a 'duffer'. Interestingly, one of the meanings of this word is 'something worthless or useless', but to us it was everything.

I remember vividly two duffers that were given to me which had a huge impact on my life. Both were when I was about 15 years old. The first was when about six of us were round a girl's house, trying to impress her and her mates. We had all been drinking our token can of lager or bottle of cider between the six of us. So when we were leaving the house one of my friends shouted, 'Follow the leader.' This was a command for the rest of us to do whatever he decided to do. It could be banging on someone's door or window, or something else.

As he ran away from the house with the girls looking on, he decided to jump over a car. Not just any car but a bright yellow Lotus Elite. So he jumped on the bonnet and ran over the top, leaping off the back end, closely followed by the rest of us. Two, three, four, five were all over cleanly, waiting and watching for me, but my foot slipped and landed on the windscreen. A huge crack appeared just as someone looked from behind their curtains and saw us all standing around the car and me still on it.

We all ran down the street and split up in various directions, as the owner of the car began driving down the street after us. We were never caught, but our underpants needed to be changed swiftly when we arrived at our homes.

The second occasion was when I was going out with a girl named Charlotte (not her real name) who I was really fond of. We had been going out with each other for over a year. Every Tuesday evening, my mates and I would go to Mowden Park Rugby Club disco, which was specially put on for under 18s. We used to have a great time dancing, watching others, having a laugh and snogging.

Duffered

This particular evening a group of us were walking home when I was asked by one of my mates if I had fondled Charlotte's breasts yet. My silence and embarrassment answered his question, which he then started to tease me about. He 'duffered' me to do so.

As we walked home we had to cross a field where Charlotte and I started to kiss, and before she could do anything I put my hand up her blouse and touched one of her breasts. Immediately, she pulled away and began crying and ran off home. I ran after her to apologize but she told me to get lost. I felt such a prat. I had given in once again to peer pressure and ended up regretting it, but more importantly, hurting someone I cared for.

I'm telling these stories to illustrate how easily we are affected by what others think of us, and how we often do what they want in order to be accepted by them. This attitude easily flows into the church and affects how we behave as Christians. A friend of mine was encouraged to become a local preacher in the Methodist Church many years ago. Every time he got into the pulpit to preach he would faint. This happened about three times and every time he came round a bunch of ladies were splashing water over his face and giving him a drink. I remember asking him whether God might be trying to say something to him. He realized later that he should not be preaching.

Shortly after I became a Christian, I felt that there was a calling on my life to communicate the good news of Jesus. However, it seemed that I didn't fit the mould. I now realize that God wants us to be ourselves and to allow him to make us what we should be and not what the church wants us to be or thinks we should be.

I have always wanted to be open to bring God's message in whatever way he chooses. Unfortunately I have made mistakes in the past and no doubt will in the future, but I hope I will be humble enough to admit this and repent where needed and apologize when required. When you get to this point in your Christian life, you put yourself in a position of being misunderstood or written off by other Christians. This is why it is important to be accountable to people and have true friends who will love, protect and correct you.

In the last eight years or so I think I have started to discover how some of the biblical characters must have felt, especially the prophets, due to some of their bizarre behaviour in bringing God's message. In 1995 an American couple came to Sheffield and prophesied over my wife and me. Part of the word was, 'And though your actions seem bizarre now, some in the future will seem even more bizarre because there is a proclamation of prophecy that needs to be seen.' As this was spoken over us, I got very excited and shouted and jumped up and down. This was not because I felt important or special. It was because I felt

God was encouraging me by saying, 'It's OK, you are on the right track; you have not lost your marbles.'

When I began to carry a stick around with me, either to worship God or pray with, this always caused a stir among the Christians. I went to a city-wide prayer event, where there must have been up to 300 people. I had been in the meeting about five minutes when a leader came up to me and asked if I would put the stick down. So I politely asked why. His response was, 'Because we do not have a theology for sticks!' Isn't it funny how, as soon as we (myself included) don't understand something of what God is doing, we try to theologize it rather than talking to the people concerned?

If you were to come to my house, you would see that I have a basket-load of sticks, of all sizes and shapes, in my dining-room, which represent different things to help me when I pray. I have a stick which represents healing, and another with people's names on it so I can hold it and pray for the people on the stick. I was given a stick by a friend in Leeds, so when I use that I pray for the city of Leeds.

For a long time I would stand or dance around a Union Jack, banging my stick in the middle of the flag. A few months after I had been doing this, I felt God gave me understanding of what was happening. He told me that for every time I hit the flag with the stick, it would represent another person entering the kingdom of God. As you can imagine, I began to bang louder and more frequently. Sometimes I felt I should press the end of the stick gently into the stomach of the person I had been asked to pray for, as God was saying he wanted to do a deep work within that person.

Kum ba ya

While in America on holiday, I was given a stick at a friend's church barbecue. In their Sunday meeting the next day, during the worship our friend Bob felt God was saying that he should play a song on the drums and sing. Bob is part of the worship team of the church, and we were to find out later that he has never done this before or since. He told the church he was going to sing 'Kum ba ya my Lord', and Linda and I looked at each other as if to ask, 'Did I really hear him right?'

What made it more embarrassing was what he said next. He told the church that while he was singing and playing, Baz was going to come out and dance with his stick in front of everyone, as God was going to do something significant for the church that morning. I could not believe what I was hearing! I was going to have to dance to a song I've mocked so many times. How could I dance to that song in a manly way?

As Bob encouraged me at the front of the church, all I could say to God was, 'Please help me.' I stood facing the church, nervously waiting for Bob to start and wondering what these lovely people were thinking. As Bob began to play, I was surprised and rejoicing that the rhythm he was playing was not that of our Sunday school tune but something like an African tribal dance. As he began to sing in a slow and deliberate way, I felt the Holy Spirit anoint me and I began to dance. I have been using sticks to worship God for a number of years now, as this helps me to do so in a masculine way. This Sunday was no exception; I felt free to be a warrior dancing to and for my God. What happened next surprised Bob, the leaders and me. A few people began to run to the front of the church.

They were crying, kneeling, lying down, and the noise was staggering as people began to pray out loud, 'God, come by here – please don't pass us by!' People did business with God that morning.

One gentleman named George asked if he could use my stick. As I gave it to him, he shouted out, 'Men, get hold of this stick, as it represents authority.' As the men came and touched the stick, George prayed for them. Ultimately, it is the Holy Spirit who helps us in our prayers.[67]

I brought back a stick (similar to a Moses-type staff) last week from Romania to assist me in my prayers for a friend and the work he is doing among street children. I find it helps me to focus more easily on what I'm praying for as I hold the stick or worship. Standing on a hillside overlooking Sheffield, I feel I can pray and intercede for the city far more passionately with a stick in my hand than without. This does not mean my prayers are more effective than anyone else's – it just means this is right for me and helpful. When I first began taking sticks into church meetings people were wary, sceptical and cynical. One lady from the church I attended wrote to me saying how she initially related it to American Indian rain dances and totem poles and did not feel it had much to do with God. However, after talking to one of her friends, her opinion changed. Her friend had informed her that when I banged the stick next to her, she felt a real outpouring of the Holy Spirit. She went on to say that she realized God was saying I needed to bring the sticks into the church as a prophetic statement of what God was doing and is to do in the nation.

In the same year, I went to hear two Baptist ministers associated with Toronto Airport Fellowship in Canada. They shared about their spiritual journey and what God had done in their lives and where he was taking them. What was to follow was to shock and encourage me at the same time.

During the meeting I had the weird thought that I should pull the heads off the flower display at the front of the church and throw the petals over these two men. I told my friend what I thought and he just smiled at me.

Later on there was an opportunity for us to ask these guys any questions about what they had been talking about or anything to do with what God was doing in these days. Many questions were being asked and I thought I would ask them the following:

'Have you come across people in your travels who are doing some strange things in the whole area of prophecy, such as symbolism and acting out things to bring God's message to individuals or churches?'

The reason for asking this was that once again I was feeling vulnerable about what God was doing with me and asking of me.

Their response was affirmative. But what was to follow was to shock and encourage me at the same time. Rick (one of the guys) replied, 'God has told you to say and do something over us, hasn't he?'

'Yes,' I replied.

'Well, you had better do it at the end of the meeting.'

My friend just looked at me and laughed!

At the close of the meeting I went up to both of these men and stood them alongside the large flower display. I had spoken to the leader of this church beforehand, explaining what I felt I should do. Feeling very apprehensive, I began to pull the heads off the flowers until most of them were in my hands. I said to these men that God wanted them to know what it meant to be the fragrance of death to some and the fragrance of life to others.[68] I then began to drop these petals on their heads. Before one touched them, they were both lying on the floor under the power of God.

All I could think of was the mess I was making on the floor, so I kept on saying, 'I'm sorry, I will hoover up after!'

People were still in the church and the looks were varied. Eventually, these two ministers got up and came to talk to me and thanked me for being obedient to God. That morning, as they were praying about their time in the UK, they informed me that they actually smelt a sweet fragrance enter the room they were praying in. Their first thought was that it must be the cleaner or the lady of the home. They soon discovered that no one else was in the house but them. God was speaking to them and he confirmed it by the flower petals. God is great!

Some time later Linda and I were praying with some of our friends at their home. I felt I should pour over the husband a large bowl of pot-pourri that was on their fireplace. I shared this with Linda to see what she thought. The husband heard me talking and said, 'Whatever God is saying, just do it.' So I picked up the bowl and began to pour this over him. As the pieces hit him, God impacted his life in a very powerful way through the Holy Spirit.

ELPIZO

A few years later I felt God speak to me about dyeing my hair blond and having the word ELPIZO (meaning 'hope') shaved in the back and dyed red. This was to represent that I was praying for God's love to spread through this nation like a forest fire. I was amazed at the reaction I got from people. One of my neighbours called me over and said, 'What the hell is that on the back of your head?' When I told her, she replied, 'We could do with a bit of that in this country.'

I only ever had one negative reaction from a non-Christian and that was when I was with some friends at a bingo hall. After being asked to explain the haircut, some of the staff reacted quite aggressively and told me that they wanted none of that stuff there. Apart from that incident, it's interesting that most of the complaints came from Christians.

Later on I kept getting the impression I should shave my head bald and just leave the word on the back. I spoke to my wife Linda about this and asked my friends what they thought, as I didn't particularly want to draw attention to myself. Linda suggested I should wait a while and see what God was trying to say through this.

A few weeks later Linda and I were at a conference for churches that were part of the network we belong to. During one of the meetings a guy got up at the front of the meeting and began to prophesy. He is well respected and trusted among our churches and recognized as a prophet. He began by saying he believed there was going to be a move among men in the whole area of humility. As a sign of this some men had already been challenged by God to shave their heads. I turned to Linda and we just smiled. It must be difficult at times for my wife to be married to someone like me!

Before I shaved my head, I decided to phone the schools that I visit on a regular basis to inform them about what I was planning on doing. I didn't want them to think I was encouraging any of the pupils to do likewise. The response I got from the schools was very interesting: none of the schools asked me not to come in while my head was bald. In the staff-room of one school a staff member made the following comment: 'At last God is doing something in the church.' People are looking for spiritual guidance, and yet we Christians can often be the stumbling-block for them, either by the way we behave or by the way we restrict God's working through us!

I wish I could say to you that every time God has asked me to do something for him, I have responded positively and been obedient. It's not that God is asking me to do some strange and wacky things every week. All I'm trying to do is to be open to him when he does speak and to be faithful to him.

About ten years ago I clearly felt God guiding me to begin to wear chains. One of the places was to be at the National Evangelists' Conference held at Swanwick every year. I felt that God wanted to remind the evangelists who attended that they were called by God to preach the good news and break the chains over people's lives through Jesus, and allow God to break any chains over their own lives that were restricting them from knowing the fullness of life in Christ.

After checking this out with the committee who plan the conference, I went to buy the chains. Please try to imagine me in Homebase, wrapping chains around myself as people passed the aisle! They were all looking at me as if I had just escaped from the film set of *One Flew Over the Cuckoo's Nest*. Once I had got enough chains, I got one of the assistants to cut them.

I felt that each delegate should be offered the chance, as part of their response to God, to take home with them a chain link to remind them of their calling, so I bought enough to have 350 links. One of the committee members kindly paid for the links.

What was so good about this conference was that right at the beginning, one of the committee members told the delegates why I was wearing the chains, and said they believed it was a prophetic statement to the conference. The speaker for the conference, Jeff Lucas, also referred to the chains during one of his sessions, which again was such a blessing. I have to admit I still felt vulnerable wearing the chains all day, especially at meal times and when we went out for a curry.

However, the way the conference delegates responded was fantastic. Not everyone took a link or fully embraced what I was doing, but I didn't get one negative comment to my face. Behind my back, I'm not so sure! Probably because evangelists are used to flack themselves, they were being sensitive to me.

During the next three to four months I wore the chains every Sunday morning at my home church. I was not sure why, but I knew I had to. One Sunday morning a friend of mine (Gary from Bournemouth) was speaking. During his talk he mentioned the prisoners in America who are on death row. When they are about to go to be executed, a guard walks in front of them shouting 'Dead man walking!' as they follow slowly behind in chains. As soon as I heard this, God said, 'That's why you are wearing these chains – to remind you and the church that there are dead men walking everywhere and you are the people to bring them back to life and free them through Jesus.'

The reason this chapter is called 'Zany Gob Case' is because it is an anagram of my name. A friend in my church discovered this a few years ago; however, I believe it is God just encouraging and reminding me that I am a fool for Christ and prepared to look a fool in others' eyes to speak out the truth for Jesus. It is not always easy living this way, but it is nothing compared to the humiliation and pain that Christ went through for you and me.

Are you willing to stand up and be counted for Jesus, whatever he asks of you? Are you willing to be a 'sign and a wonder'?

Questions

- In what ways did God ask the Old Testament prophets to communicate his message?
- How would you feel if you were in their shoes (or sandals)?
- Has God ever asked you to do something you have felt was rather odd? Did you do it?
- Have you got close friends around you to sound things out with?
- Are you accountable to anyone? If not, why not?
- Do you allow yourself to be open to the Holy Spirit to be used in new and creative ways?
- Read the gospels again and see how Jesus communicated to different people. What can you learn from this?

Die as a martyr, not out of stupidity.

Anonymous

25

How to Be a Better Husband

Baz

Surely not. Me – a good husband?

How can those of us who are married be good husbands and make sure we give enough time to our relationship and friendship with our wives? How can we make sure we don't allow work to consume our lives or our insecurities to hinder our marriages?

Firstly, you need to know this is not going to be one of those articles giving you seven points to make your marriage successful. I hate all that. One, because I am crap at maths; and two, because I always fail after point two.

I will tell how it is for me, and if you can glean anything from this, great; and if not, that's OK. Before writing this chapter, I thought I would first ask my wife Linda if she thought I was a good husband and where I could improve, and what she thought makes a good husband. She has seen the good, bad and ugly sides of me in the last fifteen years, so she could have some wisdom on this.

So this is what she said. She first suggested that men should not be harsh with their wives, especially in their speech. I see so many men inside and outside the church who speak to and of their wives as if they were some piece of dirty rag. 'Love your wives and do not be harsh with them' (Col. 3:19).

A husband should make time to get to know his wife. What are her interests? Go and do and see what she likes, and don't expect to do all you like. Talk to her about what she likes and, more importantly, listen. Listen not just with your ears but with your eyes. Guys, let's be honest – we can't multi-task, so give her your full attention. Otherwise you will hear those words, 'Are you listening to me?' And our reply 'Yes' is always followed by 'What have I just said?' You and I mumble something, which is never correct, which just causes upset, frustration and tension. Someone once said, 'The best way to listen to someone is to look at them', as this shows you are saying, 'I value you as a person and you have my total attention.' We all want to feel valued; what a great way to show it.

We all want to be encouraged, and so do our wives. This does not always have to be verbal. A smile, a wink, a hug, a kiss, a love note left under the quilt; we can all do this (and it won't cost you anything financially, for those who are stingy at spending on their wives!). And for those who like buying flowers, weekends away, flights to New York and so on, all it takes is to think of someone else rather than you! Be romantic. If you find this hard, work at it and ask your wife what she would like you to do for her. Make sure this is not just done on birthdays, anniversaries, Valentine's Day or Christmas. Learn to be spontaneous, and make sure it's not just because you want sex but because you are expressing your love and appreciation to your wife. Book date nights in your diary so nothing else can creep in, like work, friends or family.

Recognize that marriage is a partnership. We should treat our wives as equals and with respect. Gently push her and encourage her in areas where she might naturally want to back off. Don't let your insecurities and hurts make you hold your wife back and don't allow yourself to be threatened by your wife's strengths and successes. You need to learn to be yourself and not compare yourself with other men.

In all of the above, keep reminding yourself of the promises you made to your wife on your wedding day. I promised Linda that I would always believe the best about her and be faithful. I want to keep on doing this, so thanks, Linda, for reminding me of the above and how I can be the husband who will bring out the best in you.

Be confident but open.

Anonymous

26

Reality vs. Fantasy

Baz

When I was a child I talked like a child, I thought like a child, I reasoned like a child . . .
1 Corinthians 13:11

It was so easy when I was a child to lose myself in a world of fantasy. This I would do daily as I played football or ran up and down the cobbled back alley of my home, imagining that I was running out onto the pitch of Wembley in my England kit or running to the finish line in the 100 metres final of the Olympic Games.

When I was a teenager at school I still had those fantasies, but they were often pushed to the back of my mind by bigger things, such as the breasts of one of my teachers. I would often go into my own little world, wondering what it would be like to see them in the flesh and touch them.

'When I became a man I put childish ways behind me' (1 Cor. 13:11). Am I the only man who still behaves in childish ways? Every time I read that, I think, 'Man, I am so sick.' Thanks, Paul, for making me feel worse.

Why is it that when the weather improves and the skirts get shorter and the T-shirts get tighter, the childish ways manifest themselves in me? Is it because men think of sex every seven seconds, or is it because we like to enter a world of fantasy and escape from the reality going on around us and in us?

Reality is what we live in day in, day out, and is different for each one of us. For some, it can be an enormous thing to get through daily because of the tears, pain and hurt we feel due to loss, anger, fears. For others, it can just be the sense of the mundane in their lives that causes frustration, and they ask, 'Is this as good as it gets?' So to escape from these or other feelings, we try to hide away. We try to not live life in the real world and we enter a world of escapism.

Fantasy can be defined as: the realm of vivid imagination; make believe; a mental image, especially a disordered and weird image. So fantasy can be anything that takes us away from the realities and responsibilities that we have in our everyday life.

So whether we are single or married, we have to make daily choices about what we are going to let our mind do. Are we going to be ruled by our mind or are we going to take control of it? We need to ask God to help us be the men he wants us to be and believes we can be.

For us to do this, we need to be honest about our struggles and get some friends to stand alongside us as we make ourselves vulnerable and accountable to them, asking for their support and help. Whatever you turn to in order to avoid reality, ask yourself, 'What are the needs I am trying to meet?'

Now, I know for most guys, we find it hard to talk about our feelings unless we are talking about sport, cars, money or work, and then we can talk for England. However, we need to begin to open up and not allow fear to rob us of the freedom we can and will receive from God once we begin this process.

Let's be honest here. All guys in the church, single or married, struggle with lustful thoughts. Men generally, whether part of the church or not, all lust.

Sometimes, I am just about to be introduced to speak at a church, when five minutes earlier I was admiring some lady's breasts, while trying to worship God. It's true – men cannot multi-task!

Matthew Fitzgerald said, 'Lust is especially dangerous because it causes a man to think with his crotch and throw all reason and logic to the wind.'[69]

I read recently that one of the reasons why men get into the world of fantasy is anger. If you struggle with fantasizing, could it be you are angry over something, and this has caused you to look somewhere else rather than face the reality of your anger and the cause of it.

We live in a fantasy world. A world of illusion.
The great task in life is to find reality.
Iris Murdoch[70]

Reality is the quality or state of being actual or true. So for us to find reality in our lives we must be truthful to ourselves, God and some mates about what we run to when we want our escapism fix. Is it surfing the TV channels late at night when your housemates or your wife are upstairs in bed? Or is it the Internet or magazines? Or maybe it's even smoking some weed to bring some pleasure or relaxation as you begin the journey of hiding from the truth?

Earl Nightingale says: 'Whatever we plant in our subconscious mind and nourish with repetition and emotion will one day become reality.'[71] In other words: 'As we think, we are.'

When the disciples asked Jesus, 'Teach us how to pray', one aspect of the prayer was 'Lead us not into temptation' (Luke 11:1–4). Temptation: something that seduces or has the quality to seduce. The desire to have or do something that you know you should avoid.

Let's not wait until we can see or taste temptation before we cry out 'Help!' to God. Let's ask him not to let us get anywhere near it; let's recognize it quickly when it appears; let's run from our youthful desires, as Paul encourages us to do, no matter how young or old we are; let's just get the hell out of that place!

My favourite hymn is 'O Jesus I Have Promised'. Just read these amazing words and use them as your prayer to God, today:

> O Jesus I have promised to serve thee to the end.
> Be thou for ever near me, my Master and my Friend:
> I shall not fear the battle if thou art by my side,
> Nor wander from the pathway if thou wilt be my Guide.
>
> O let me feel thee near me; the world is ever near.
> I see the sights that dazzle, the tempting sounds I hear;
> My foes are ever near me, around me and within.
> But Jesus, draw thou nearer, and shield my soul from sin.
>
> O let me hear thee speaking in accents clear and still,
> Above the storms of passion, the murmurs of self will.
> O speak to reassure me, to hasten or control;
> O speak, and make me listen, thou Guardian of my soul.
>
> O Jesus, thou hast promised, to all who follow thee,
> That where thou art in glory, there shall thy servant be;
> And Jesus, I have promised to serve thee to the end.
> O give me grace to follow, my Maker and my Friend.
>
> O let me see they footmarks, and in them plant mine own.
> My hope to follow duly is in thy strength alone.
> O guide me, call me, draw me, uphold me to the end;
> And then in heaven receive me, my Saviour and my Friend.
>
>   John Ernest Bode (1816–74)

Sixteen years ago last December, Linda and I and guests sang this at our wedding, where I made a promise to my wife Linda that I would be always faithful to her and never leave her.

Well, this will only happen as I choose to continue to live in reality and not fantasy. When I do go down the road of fantasy, I need to quickly realize how dangerous this is and get myself right with God again and quickly return to the world of reality.

27

Resources for Men and Men's Groups (1): Men in Movies

Matt Page

People today go to church to be entertained, and the cinema to be challenged.
Anonymous

Few art forms have the potential to challenge us as directly as film. You probably don't have to think very hard to name a film that's left you inspired, angry, challenged or motivated to change the world. You only have to look at a chapter in this book to see the impact that *Braveheart* had on Lee and Baz. What's incredible about cinema is that even though pretty much none of us know what it is like to be a blue-woaded twelfth-century Scottish knight, the movie still spoke to many ordinary blokes about living a life after God. Somehow it communicates something that we can take and apply to our ordinary, not always thrilling, lives.

Of course it doesn't work all the time. For every film that leaves people inspired, there are probably at least ten which are nothing really special. But for anyone who's happy to lay aside the latest James Bond film in search of something a little more substantial, here's a handful of films that may make you a changed man.

Movie ministers

Firstly, let's look at some of the positive portrayals of men of faith. Christians often claim that they get a raw deal in the media, but given our track record, we don't do too badly. Let's face it – if the church had been a shining beacon of integrity for the last 2,000 years, then no one would buy the 'hypocritical Christian' stereotype. Contrary to popular belief, there are actually lots of positive portrayals of Christians in the movies, if only we look hard enough. The simplest way to depict a 'committed Christian' in cinematic shorthand is to go for some sort of Christian leader.

One of my favourites in this respect is *The Mission* which stars Jeremy Irons and Robert DeNiro as two priests trying to spread the gospel to unreached native American tribes whilst slave traders attempt to carve up the continent to line their own pockets. There's something very sobering about seeing the commitment these guys and their colleagues had to preaching the gospel, the lengths they went to and the risks they took. It also looks at how it's often harder for us to forgive ourselves than it is for God to forgive us. However, the film saves its biggest questions for the third act, as the slavers come to take the village that the priests are living in. The film refuses to tell you what to think and as a result raises up genuine questions about if, and how, the followers of the Prince of Peace should defend themselves.

A similar question is raised by the 2005 film *Joyeux Noël*, which recounts the remarkable events of the Christmas Eve ceasefire during World War I. One of the characters is a priest who feels fighting would be wrong, but who nevertheless accompanies the men from his village to the trenches as their chaplain. There's so much more in this film than this one character, as, for a brief moment, humanity triumphs over the inhumanity of the Great War's trenches.

Catholic priests have actually always been rather popular with film makers. Another classic portrayal is Father Barry from *On the Waterfront* – best known for Marlon Brando's 'I coulduh been a contenduh' speech. Whilst Brando's character is a sort of 'Christ figure', it's Father Barry who steals the show when he resolves to take on the mob and their corrupt union down at the docks. When the one person who rallies to his call to fight back is killed off, Father Barry is taunted and told to get back to his church. But, despite being pelted with garbage, he stands his ground, and, in the face of overwhelming hostility, he delivers one of my favourite speeches in the history of cinema:

> Boys, this is my church. And if you don't think Christ is down here on the waterfront you've got another guess coming. And who do you think he lines up with? Every morning when the hiring boss blows his whistle, Jesus stands alongside you in the shape up. He sees why some of you get picked and some of you get passed over. He sees the family men worrying about getting their rent and getting food in the house for the wife and kids . . . Christ is always with you. Christ is in the shape up, he's in the hatch – he's in the union hall – he's kneeling here beside Nolan – and he's saying with all of you, 'If you do it to the least of mine, you do it to me.' What they did to Joey, what they did to Nolan, they're doing to you, and you, and you. And only you, with God's help, have the power to knock 'em off for good.

Probably few of us are priests, but the mentality of calling the harshest areas near where we live our church and claiming it for God, no matter what gets thrown at us, is truly inspiring. Incidentally, another great film priest is Father Logan in Hitchcock's *I Confess*, who is prepared to stick to his principles even though it might mean he gets convicted of a murder he knows someone else committed.

More recently, other denominations have been allowed to get in on the act too. Changing language, as well as denomination, a brilliant recent film is *Italian for Beginners*. Rather than one or two lead actors, this features an 'ensemble cast' of nine actors who all live in a small town and gradually become friends. Most of them have lived for years in the town, the one exception being Andreas, the new, temporary, pastor of the dead-on-its-feet local church.

Suffice to say that if our church was ever after a new church leader, I would give this guy the job. Many would choose to moan about a post where they had to live out of a suitcase, and where their congregation dips below three, but instead, Andreas takes it as an opportunity to get out and meet the broken people around him. His approachability and his gentle humour put them at ease and help them open up to him.

Andreas doesn't have the steely defiance of Father Barry, but is still a man of great strength. The pain of his wife's recent death is tangible and it is a very real obstacle for his faith. But the film shows him rejecting being a victim and finding his feet again as he helps others find theirs. His pain is an obstacle, but it's one he is determined to shift or get around. It's not a Hollywood film, and so there are no dramatic 'I will not be a victim!' speeches, but that only makes it feel more real. And although the subtleties of what is really happening take a few viewings to emerge, the humanity, warmth, approachability and humour are much clearer from the start. It's great to see a film showing someone living with the reality of faith, reaching out to people, and in this case seeing the fruit of it.

Often some of the best portrayals of faith start out quite negatively, before the character in question learns something that changes them and challenges us in the process. A recent example of this is the biting US Christian high-school satire *Saved!* It has been much criticized in Christian circles, and it's certainly not an evangelist's dream-film-come-true. Nevertheless, more Christians need to see it, because the satire is so spot on in places that it causes you to question some of the absurdities of the Christian world (even whilst you're laughing so hard that you choke on your popcorn).

As the film is based in a Christian school, nearly all the characters would identify themselves as Christians, and yes, in this case many of them are shallow or hypocritical. The most interesting character in the film, for me at least, is the head-teacher of the school, Pastor Skip (played by Martin Donovan). At the start of the film Skip is the worst kind of youth worker. Speaking like he's recently swallowed a copy of the *Street Bible*, and trying fancy tricks to impress his students, he is as cringe-worthy and as shallow as he is annoyingly familiar.

But as the film unwinds we find out that his exterior masks the turmoil of a failing marriage, and a people-less legalistic belief system that is gradually failing to hold everything together. Yet, as the film veers to its (perhaps overly comfortable) happy ending, our last view of Skip shows him finally beginning to be real, and wrestling with some of the difficulties and contradictions that life has thrown his way. It's a masterful shot, and whilst the overall view of the film-makers is somewhat questionable, they manage to find a humanity in Skip whilst (hopefully) challenging those like him.

Another example of the bad-Christian-comes-good film is Robert Duvall's *The Apostle*. Duvall plays an evangelist who runs away from his church after committing a crime, and tries to rebuild his life by carrying on in the only career he knows – preaching. This is probably a scenario alien to most of us, especially as it is set in America's Deep South, but the way that Duvall's salvation is found gradually, as he actually shares his life in community with those around him, is a lesson for us all. It's not the easiest film to relate to, but there is plenty in it to make you think.

'Ordinary Christians'

Thankfully, not all of the Christians we have seen in the cinema are professionals and, as most of those reading this book are probably not ordained ministers, you'll be pleased to know that I want to highlight a few 'ordinary Christians' as well (although, let's face it, Christians should never be merely ordinary).

Perhaps the most famous and best-loved example is Eric Liddell in *Chariots of Fire*. The story of *Chariots of Fire* is all the more extraordinary because it's based on real events, and perhaps it's also a little too easy to get carried away with it because ultimately Liddell won. What is strange about the film is how many modern-day Christians, who would happily go for a kick-about or buy something from a shop on a Sunday, still relate to it. I'm a rugby player myself, and whilst my team plays predominantly on Saturdays, I've still been OK playing the odd game on a Sunday. Yet somehow I still love the film.

The reason *Chariots of Fire* works, and is so beloved even by those who don't share Liddell's theology, is because it fundamentally understands how intricately connected Liddell's faith and his athletic performance are. There are very few films that do this. As the Duke of Sutherland says at one point, 'The "lad", as you call him, is a true man of principles and a true athlete. His speed is a mere extension of his life, its force. We sought to sever his running from himself.'

Have you ever wondered if Liddell would have won if he had gone against his conscience? I can't help feeling he might not have done. Not because God is mean and nasty and would want to teach him a lesson, but simply because our faith is holistic and you can't separate Eric-the-Christian from Eric-the-athlete. The earlier scene where he drags himself up after a fall and still wins the race is a key one. The determination he shows there, which ultimately wins him his gold, comes from his inner conviction that God has made him fast and the knowledge that when he runs, he feels God's pleasure.

So, given that many of this book's readers will not share Liddell's views on the Sabbath, and that most of us won't be racing in the Olympics, what can we take from the film? Well, firstly, that our principles are important. Our world is becoming increasingly driven by 'what works' rather than what is right, and it's easy for us to sacrifice our principles to get a result (which can happen in church things as well as, say, normal work). It's far too tempting not to trust God in these things and just to do what needs doing to get a result. That wasn't what Liddell did. He counted it as nothing, and threw it away, knowing that what God said was more important than getting earthly results. Thankfully, Liddell won, but it's important to realize that he didn't know that when he made the decision. And in reality, even if we make the right choice, we won't necessarily get the result we want. Watching *Chariots of Fire* back to back with *The Mission* would probably give a good perspective on things. Doing the right thing is not always successful, but it is always the right thing.

That conviction is also shared by the witty and articulate Thomas More in *A Man for All Seasons*. Refusing to go the along with the church's split from Rome, he finds himself on the wrong side of Henry VIII's cronies. It would have been easy for More to follow the advice he was given to 'say it with your mouth but renounce it in your head', but he knew that would violate his integrity – something he ultimately pays for with his life.

Another Christian with an extraordinary talent with words was the writer C.S. Lewis. Two versions of Lewis's life, or rather how Lewis dealt with finding love and then losing it again, have been made in the last twenty years. Interestingly, they emphasize quite different elements of Lewis's character. Norman Stone's BAFTA-winning BBC film *Shadowlands* (1985) paid particular attention to his normality, and his Christianity. On the other hand, Richard Attenborough's 1993 film of the same name stresses the wit and wisdom that made Lewis so popular as a Christian writer. It's hard to choose which film is better. The later film looks nicer, and Hopkins gives a more dynamic performance, but the earlier one stays with Lewis that bit longer, to the point where he rediscovers his faith.

One of my favourite film portrayals of a Christian in recent years is the police officer Jim Kurring in *Magnolia*. This is a tough film to watch, and many balk at the early scene where Tom Cruise leads a non-Christian version of a *Cut to the Chase* seminar. But it's worth pushing through, because redemption is at its most powerful when it overcomes the biggest obstacles. The Prodigal Son wasn't a story about a nice kosher boy who just got a bit bored with the synagogue, but about a man who wished his father dead so he could squander his money on booze and sex, and then defiled himself further by working with 'unclean' pigs.

Magnolia is another film with no obvious lead actors, and it set a new trend in film-making by interweaving the seemingly unrelated lives of numerous individuals into one big story. Kurring is one such character. What's great about him is that he's so ordinary. Many of the above characters are professionals: Lewis possessed a brilliant mind; Liddell was a super-athlete with an obvious divine gift. Kurring is just a normal police officer and not even a particularly good one – he even loses his gun in one scene. But he is a good man, honest, and equally determined to live for God. And as such he acts as a channel that God uses to pour his grace into the lives of two of the most lost people in the whole film. I suspect that if you had asked Liddell which the greater achievement was, he would have willingly swapped places.

Sometimes, as Christians, we can be guilty of wanting Hollywood to represent us as something we aren't – as super-infallible Christians, rather than normal people with our own shortcomings. *Magnolia* certainly never falls into that trap and, as such, depicts a man we can relate to now, rather than the man we would like to be but never will be.

'Character' is very much the focus of *The Big Kahuna*, a film based on a play, starring Kevin Spacey and Danny DeVito. Spacey and DeVito play Larry and Phil, two experienced salesmen at a sales convention who team up with the company new boy, Bob (Peter Facinelli), in an attempt to win a major contract. At first it seems that they have utterly failed. The big executive didn't even turn up – or so it seemed. But as they conduct a postmortem on their failed operation, Bob realizes that not only did the man in question put in an appearance, but Bob had even had the chance to speak to him. But when they discover that Bob had used most of his time with this man to evangelize him, rather than sell him the industrial lubricants as he was meant to, Larry and Phil are understandably annoyed.

Is Jesus more important than industrial lubricants? Of course. (Did I really need to ask?) But should Bob be selling the gospel when he's meant to doing his job? To be honest, even after several viewings, I'm still not sure. But that's the kind of wonderful ambiguity you get with art. And although the writer and director want you to see the world as DeVito does, I can't help wondering if the film somehow breaks free from what they intended, and supports Bob far more than they realized.

One final example that combines both pro and amateur Christians is the film version of *Les Miserables* starring Liam Neeson as Jean Valjean. Musical haters need not fear – there are no songs here, as this is based on the book only, and it reminds you of what a great story it was before it became such a popular musical.

For anyone who doesn't know the story, it begins with an incredible act of grace, and shows how that event completely changes Valjean's life, who in turn lives a life of sheer goodness. There are other versions of it around, but the emphasis this one puts on that initial act, and Neeson at his best, make this one worth watching again and again.

Non-Christians

Of course, men who aren't Christians can also be inspirational – just look at Gandhi – and the cinema has produced so many examples that I can only concentrate on a few.

For some reason, film Christians are never inspirational as fathers, whereas there are a good number of great father figures in the cinema in general. Perhaps the best recent example is Johnny from *In America*. Johnny is staggering his way through the loss of a child and the pressures of trying to start a new life in a new country whilst trying to provide for his wife and three kids. It's an incredible example of everyday heroism, and being extraordinary in the ordinary stuff of life.

Another great film father can be found in Roberto Benigni's *Life is Beautiful*. Benigni plays Guido, a Jewish man who marries and has a son in the years just before the outbreak of the Second World War. When the Germans invade Italy, Guido's family are sent to a concentration camp. Guido manages to convince his son that this is all a game, and if they play the game correctly they will win a big prize. It's an unbelievable example of the totally selfless love and sacrifice of a father to protect his son. Incredibly, it manages to be heart-warming and heartbreaking at the same time. Some have questioned whether Guido is right to trick his son in order to save his life, but I think that misses the point. What is most powerful about the film is the way Guido sidelines his own raw fear and terror in order to preserve his son. If you've never cried at a film, this might be the one that finally breaks you.

If you really want to delve into the father theme, there are plenty of films to see. Atticus Finch in *To Kill a Mockingbird*, Marlon in *Finding Nemo*, Giuseppe Conlon in *In the Name of the Father*, and Anakin Skywalker in er . . . no, hang on. Hopefully, you get the picture anyway.

For those of us who aren't dads yet, thankfully Hollywood has given us many other inspiring characters whose example we can follow. Both Russell Crowe and Al Pacino's characters in *The Insider* deserve a mention for the way they risk their lives, their careers, and, in Crowe's case, the security of their families, in order to defeat a real-life evil empire. Oscar Schindler in *Schindler's List* is a hero not so much for his risk-taking as his cunning, his ingenuity and his compassion. And whilst Lee's very keen on *Braveheart* and its emphasis of 'Freeeeedooom', I've always preferred the more just, and proportionate, lead character in *Rob Roy*. (What is it with Liam Neeson's characters?)

Non-men!

Of course, as my friend Stu Jesson pointed out, 'Must the only characters who inspire us to be good men, be men themselves?' To which the answer is, of course not. The original *Dead Men Walking* book was so called partly because of the film *Dead Man Walking* where Sister Helen Prejean mixes deep compassion with firm conviction. Her certainty that confession and forgiveness not only matter, but are crucial, and her willingness to endure harsh personal comments even from the man she is trying to save, are a great example, particularly in a society hooked on relativism and revenge.

Other female role models who can spur us on to be better men include the mind-blowingly generous Babette from *Babette's Feast*, whose extravagant celebration of God's provision offers a great parable of God's grace; the unconditional and redemptive love of Lena in *Punch Drunk Love*; and Marge Gunderson's victory of decency over greed and deceit in *Fargo*. However, my personal favourite is Paikea in *Whale Rider*. She grabs hold of the call she believes there is on her life, and holds on, regardless of the opposition she faces, until it comes to pass.

And I suppose you can also be inspired by non-humans: Sam's faithfulness and loyalty in the *Lord of the Rings* trilogy; Spock's sacrifice in *Star Trek: The Wrath of Khan*; and Night Crawler reciting bits of the Bible to help him overcome his fears in *X-Men 2*. And there's a certain lion in a small film you might have heard of called *The Lion, The Witch and the Wardrobe* – and yes, he's voiced by Liam Neeson.

Questions

- What inspires you to become a better man?
- Which films have achieved that for you?
- What films have challenged you or caused you to change an opinion?
- Which film character best sums you up?
- Why not rent one of the films above the next time you are with your mates, and resist the temptation to get *Bad Boys/Bond/Blade* again? Take a risk!

Resources

- *Christianity Today* – the website that expands on the magazine has a whole film section with reviews of pretty much every film on general release from some top reviewers: www.christianitytoday.com/movies
- www.artsandfaith.com – an online discussion forum with a major emphasis on film, and a top 100 of spiritually significant films.
- *How Movies Helped Save My Soul: Finding Spiritual Fingerprints in Culturally Significant Films* – a book by Gareth Higgins (Relevant Books, 2003).
- *Through a Screen Darkly* – a book by Jeffrey Overstreet (Regal Books, 2007).
- Matt Page's website – http://biblefilms.blogspot.com

28

Resources for Men and Men's Groups (2): Found in Translation

Matt Page

For the word of God is living and active.
Sharper than any double-edged sword.
Hebrews 4:12

It's a much-loved quote, but the real question is this: if the Bible is such a sharp, sharp sword, how come no one ever seems to do themselves an injury with it these days? When the author of Hebrews used this simile, he was thinking of a sword as a dangerous weapon. But somehow we've got to the point where the biggest risk the majority of Christians face from their Bibles is a paper cut. Rather than being 'living and powerful', our swords are either sat rusting in their scabbards, or are blunter than a tactless Northern comic.

There are a number of reasons why this is so. I'm not saying that every word is riveting, or that I never struggle with reading the Bible. I just want to suggest a few ways we can get more out of it. I suspect many people try just reading it, and maybe reading some books about the Bible, but when they find that that doesn't really work for them, they give up rather than trying anything different. And mainly that is because, if churches teach people how to read their Bibles at all, it is generally geared towards people who like words and reading books, rather than those who don't. And to be honest, for many blokes, trying something more 'creative' sounds like it's either for girls, or at the very least, blokes with wet handshakes and Frank Spencer-style clothes.

Why do we read the Bible so boringly?

Firstly, what exactly is with the 'Bible voice' that every single Christian on the planet seems to have? It's like years ago there was a world churches' convention where the different denominations realized that they didn't agree on communion, or the Bible, or whether to have hymns or choruses, and so panicked into trying to find at least one thing they could all agree on. And finally they plumped for reading the Bible in the most boring monotone possible.

I can only think we do it because we think it sounds holy, and respectful to God, but I honestly can't think of a bigger slap in the face than draining all the life and passion out of it. When Paul said he wished his opponents would castrate themselves (Gal. 5:12), did he really sound like John Major reading out the phone book?

Actually, most of the Bible was written to be read out, and funnily enough, you find that if you read it out correctly (i.e. in the same normal way you would say anything else), it makes a lot more sense. Reading the Bible like this isn't quite as easy as using the Bible Monotone Voice. It takes a bit of work, and a bit of practise, and is a bit more risky, but it is so much better. All you really need to do is emphasize the bits you would emphasize if you were saying those words for real. Pause occasionally. And when you come to a bit that expresses an emotion — express it, be it love or hate, joy or anger. It can help to imagine the writer in the room saying it to you. What would they sound like? Which brings us on to . . .

Imagining being there

A simple but effective way to get into parts of the Bible more is to imagine being at the place, either when the events unfolded or when the writer was writing them. So you picture being in that place and then 'look around' to see what you see, imagining the different elements that the text says were present.

So say you're looking at the passage about the raising of Lazarus. You picture being in that place, in Bethany. What was the atmosphere like? What did you feel when Lazarus died? What were the sounds of wailing like? What was the temperature like in that place? How did the atmosphere change when Jesus arrived? What did he look like? Did you expect to see him cry? Just how badly did it smell when they rolled away the stone? How did people respond to that? How did you feel when you saw Lazarus alive? What different reactions were there in the crowd?

Easy, isn't it? It's worth thinking your way around the five senses and the different stages of the story. Sometimes it's also helpful to pretend to be one of the characters – for example, a disciple. Or perhaps, in this case, even Lazarus himself. This can work well in a group setting as well: you all do it individually and then discuss who was which character.

Imagining the writer

Of course, this doesn't work so well for bits of the Bible that aren't stories. In these cases, though, I've found it helps a lot to imagine the actual writer. What would they probably have been like? The beauty of it is that the more you read it, the better your image becomes. But to get you started, here are a couple of important Bible people.

Paul

My understanding of Paul's letters got a lot better once I started to imagine him speaking his letters. Paul seems to fit a classic Jewish stereotype (even though many other Jewish people most certainly don't). He is passionate, excitable, very black-and-white, and loves to debate. He probably would have dictated most of his letters, and you can imagine him pacing around the room, with words gushing out of his mouth as some poor scribe tries to keep up. His letters are full of tangents where he gets so carried away with what he's saying that he completely goes off on one.

There are some great examples of the intense feeling he has about what he is writing. Mark Goodacre notes how Paul is so agitated and intense at the end of Galatians that he snatches the pen out of the scribe's hand and writes the last few verses in great big letters to get the point across to these 'foolish Galatians' (Gal. 6:11; 3:1).

Actually Galatians is a great place to start, as it's Paul at his most passionate and expressive. As noted above, he talks of his opponents going all the way and castrating themselves. It's not anger for anger's sake, but because he realizes how amazing the gospel of grace is, and how terrible it is that some people are trying to replace it. Paul was a man who got into trouble easily because he was totally fearless, and he was willing to cause offence when it was necessary.

It ain't those parts of the Bible that I can't understand that bother me, it's the parts that I do understand.
Mark Twain (1835–1910)

Jesus

Yeah, we all know that he didn't really have blue eyes, but most of the time we fail to picture Jesus as a Jew. The TV film *Jesus of Nazareth* does a great job of showing Jesus' dad Joseph as a typical Jewish man of that era, even giving him side-curls, but when it comes to Jesus, we're given a white European with a posh voice.

Like Paul, Jesus had a very exaggerated form of speech. 'If your right hand causes you to sin, cut it off!' (Matt. 5:30). Jesus wasn't wanting the disciples to mutilate themselves, he was simply making a point strongly. It was a classic form of teaching within Judaism at that time. He was also very passionate. He weeps at Lazarus's tomb (John 11:35). Later he cries over Jerusalem (Luke 19:41). There's a recent film called *Man Dancin'* where this Glaswegian ex-gangster gets hold of a Bible and begins to realize what Jesus actually said. There's a great scene where he recites the seven woes (Matt. 23) in front of a mirror, his eyes bulging as he reads the words.

Another great clip is the Sermon on the Mount scene from the BBC's *Son of Man*, which gets Jesus to deliver the words as he actually might have said them before they got crystallized into the form we have today. However, this leads me more into the next area I want to look at – using films to look at Scripture.

The Bible and film

I read Philip Yancey's *The Jesus I Never Knew* about five years ago, and it inspired me greatly. Yancey uses clips from the many Jesus films as a springboard to discussing particular passages. So I set out to do likewise, and gradually bought a number of films. I quickly realized how powerful this was. Whilst no film gives you a 'how it really was', they come at it from all kinds of different angles, and they opened my eyes to things in the text that I had never really seen before. The best films actually challenge some of the (often unbiblical) notions we have about Jesus, as well as fleshing out the look and feel of what it was like to be there.

Unsurprisingly, it works for other films about the Bible as well. In an age where the Bible is unknown, and people are more and more used to getting their information from visuals, this is a great way to engage with the Bible. There are a stack of images that go well with creation – the opening scene from the 1966 film *The Bible*, for starters. The recent *Bible Collection* series is also very useful, although some films (*Jeremiah, Esther*) are much better than others (*Samson and Delilah*).

A few words of caution. It's always worth comparing the films back to the original text. Film-makers often introduce their own elements. Secondly, some Bible films are poorly made – don't be too disappointed if you watch one and it does nothing for you. In fact, it's better to watch several anyway. That way, one film doesn't overly influence how you see Jesus.

I run the Bible Films Blog (Google it!), which has lists of films based on the Bible, news of Bible-based films that are in production and various reviews. I've also written a five-evening course on Jesus Films – you can download the notes from my Blog.

Comic imagination

There's one Bible film that most Christians love, even though many feel guilty for doing so – *Monty Python's Life of Brian*. What is so brilliant about *Life of Brian* is the way it uses humour to cut through the thick religious gloss that has been painted over the Bible through the years. So take, for example, the ten lepers in Luke 17:11–19. The fact is that nine of them didn't even say thank you for the incredible healing God had done in them. It's also true that sometimes people place a lot of security in their weaknesses, so healing can have a cost, and desiring it can have a price.

The ungrateful leper scene in *Life of Brian* illustrates this brilliantly. This absurd version of the story makes us reflect on how crazy it is that those nine didn't stop to say thanks, and that being healed is better than not being healed. There's plenty more to think on in the film. *Life of Brian* is one of the few Jesus films that actually showed people who were fairly neutral in their feelings for Jesus – they neither loved nor hated him. Finally, who would ever have considered the people at the back during Jesus' sermons if it hadn't been for this film?

Thinking about *Life of Brian*'s success made me realize how powerful comedy is in helping us grasp more of the reality of the Bible. Finding the humour and idiosyncrasies that are present in it can transport us closer to the actual events. By inhabiting the story and looking at it for things we find funny, we also pick up a few real truths in the process. Of course, a number of preachers have been doing this for years. I'll never forget the guy in our church who described the ending of Job as 'a bit Hollywood'.

The thing is, there's plenty of humour in the Bible already. There's a great bit of sarcasm in Isaiah 44:13–16. The story of Ehud in Judges 3 is a wonderful mix of slapstick and black comedy. Of course, there's a stack of puns that we don't get because they don't work as well in English as they do in Hebrew, but much of the Bible's natural humour is there – we just don't expect it. Many people don't expect God to be into having a laugh, but forget that he created the mechanism that makes us laugh, and the endorphins which make us feel good when we do so. And many people look down on sarcasm as either unnecessarily cruel, or as the 'lowest form of wit', despite the fact that one of God's longest speeches in the whole Bible – chapters 38 to 41 of Job – is four chapters of the purest sarcasm you will ever encounter. I love it. 'Job, was that you who created the world . . . ? Oh, no – that was me!'

The thing is that the humour in the Bible isn't there by mistake, or just to relieve the boredom. It's been intentionally chosen as the best way to communicate that particular passage. So look for it next time you read the Bible, and if you can't find any, then try looking at it through the eyes of Eddie Izzard, Ricky Gervais or whoever your favourite comedian is, and see what new angles that gives you.

> *If Christians would really live according to the teachings of Christ,*
> *as found in the Bible, all of India would be Christian today.*
> Mohandas Gandhi (1869–1948)

Bloke Art

I suspect that many blokes see art as the preserve of women in flowery Laura Ashley dresses, or the elderly stars of *Watercolour Challenge*. Fortunately, the last fifteen years have seen all that change, with the birth of what I've affectionately nicknamed 'Bloke Art'. Take Damien Hirst,[72] for example. No twee paintings of lovely bunches of lilac pansies for our Damien. Instead he says to himself, 'I know – I'll cut a cow in half and stick it in a huge vat of formaldehyde.' That's Bloke Art.

Art over the last century has gradually moved away from simply being about making something that looks like something else, to being about communication and ideas. There's two aspects to this. Firstly, art is about the artist exploring ideas, or expressing what they feel about something. Hirst, who identifies himself as a lapsed Catholic, has made several works about God, religious imagery and us. For example, he made a piece called *Adam and Eve (Banished from the Garden)* which brings home the relationship between the fall and our own mortality.

The other aspect of art is the effect it has on the viewer. An art work can communicate something new to someone, or make them think about a certain issue, even if it wasn't what was intended by the artist. In his work *Divided*, Hirst cut a cow and a calf in two, preserving each half in formaldehyde-filled glass cases. Viewers could walk between the cases. It sounds a bit gross, and yet it's actually not a million miles from the process that the Old Testament priests went through. Our religious veneer distances us from the reality of the seemingly strange way that people used to worship. It's not the main thing

Hirst is seeking to explore in his work, but many people have made the connection.

Two other, slightly less gross, bloke artists with an interest in religious images are Mark Wallinger and Simon Patterson, both of whom have made art about football. Wallinger is perhaps best known outside of art circles for his sculpture of Jesus, *Ecce Homo*. This is probably the finest piece of religious art made in the last century. Originally made to stand in Trafalgar Square, it is a life-sized 'marble' sculpture of Jesus as he stood before Pilate. The sculpture's shaved head makes him very much a Jesus for today.

As it was displayed in Trafalgar Square, it made it very much art out there rather than in stuffy galleries – a Jesus of the people. This was emphasized further by the small size of it compared to all the other statues in Trafalgar Square. It brought home the amazing fact that God became just a man and the proud empires of men were permitted to tower over him.

Art isn't just for 'artists', but for all those who are made in the image of the Creator. It's about wrestling, struggling, battling and exploring the stuff of life. If that's not something men should be doing, then I don't know what is. And as these 'bloke artists' have shown, art can use any material, and look at any issue in a new way. So why not give something a try some time and leave *Watercolour Challenge* for some other sucker?

Study

Exploring the Bible through art is not exactly a new thing. In fact, for a large chunk of church history the majority of the church hasn't been able to read, and so images have been essential to educate those who couldn't read the Bible for themselves. However, for those who could read, studying the Bible, and the research others have done on it, has always been an important building block.

Study is not always quick to produce results, but it has been significant in making the Bible more accessible, often in ways we don't understand. The last 200 years have seen things move on a great deal – often far more than most people realize. For example, we have found out how Revelation, whilst very bizarre for us to read, was written in a style that was very conventional in the day when it was written. It wasn't meant to be an obscure text for its originally intended audience, but without studying it you're never going to get what it's going on about.

We've also realized just how diverse Judaism was in Jesus' time. Rather than there being one accepted form, there were several major strands and opposing viewpoints. There was real tension between the Sadducees, who were rich and powerful because they were in Rome's pocket, and the Zealots, who wanted to overthrow the Romans and kill as many as possible until that time came. Then there were the Pharisees who disagreed with both groups and amongst themselves, and the Essenes who considered all the others so corrupt that they started afresh out in the desert. This kind of information helps us flesh out what was actually happening in the Bible, as it was written. Commentaries, Bible handbooks and dictionaries, and study Bibles are also useful here. Also useful are the kind of Christian books which look more at what the Bible is and how to read/study it, rather than the type which focus just on one issue (a bit like this one!).

Study is not easy, particularly as you often find that people disagree on issues, but it is rewarding and helps the Bible make a lot more sense than it would do otherwise.

I have known ninety-five of the world's great men in my time, and of these eighty-seven were followers of the Bible. The Bible is stamped with a Speciality of Origin, and an immeasurable distance separates it from all competitors.
W. E. Gladstone (1809–98)

Reclaiming the language of the Bible

Have you ever wondered if first-century Israel had the poshest fishermen of all time? You get these guys who were looked down on at the time by those who had been educated, because they were ignorant, and yet suddenly they start speaking in nicely cultured words.

In fact, much of the original language of the Bible has been toned down to make it appeal more to the middle classes who have tended to make up the majority of the church for most of the last 2,000 years. For the most part it was actually written in an everyday tongue, and in places it is coarser than we often care to admit.

Take, as an extreme example, Philippians 3. Paul is at pains to stress how utterly worthless the old expression of his faith was compared to knowing Christ and what he has done. The word used here is *skubalon*, which translated originally as 'dung' (KJV), then as merely 'refuse', and more recently as the even blander 'garbage' (NLT). *The Message* at least gives us 'dog dung'. But the whole point of the word *skubalon* was that it was a 'vulgar' word. There was another, more respectable, word that Paul could have used, but he deliberately went for a vulgar one. In other words, a better translation is that Paul considered all these things 'crap'. In some contexts – for example, where that word is not considered vulgar – an even stronger word might be the most appropriate translation. Yet for some reason we figure that people might be offended by using either of these words, so they get toned down, completely missing the point that Paul chose that word precisely so he could be somewhat offensive.

I'm not advocating swearing, but I am saying it's wrong to sap the Bible of its original force merely because of social niceties, and to replace realism and roughness with respectability.

Another example of this toning down is the various places in 1 Samuel and Jeremiah where the word *naba* has often been blandly translated 'prophesy' rather than 'be in a prophetic frenzy', which is much less comfortable.

Study can help dig some of these meanings out, as can using a range of translations. Get as many different translations as possible and hear the passage from each. What does each translation bring out or emphasize that the others don't? It's best to leave a gap between reading each one to let the differences sink in, rather than just trying to find a favourite translation.

To be fair, many translations do give words their full force when they could have opted for something blander. The problem is that rather than getting closer to the true meanings, some more recent translations seem to toning down earlier versions. (The King James Version is possibly the starkest of all — look up Deuteronomy 23:2 and 2 Kings 18:27 if you don't believe me!) This is a worrying trend, but one that I suppose was always going to happen once we ended up in the situation we are in, where selling Bibles is a competitive business. Anything too controversial is bad for business. For now the NRSV is probably the riskiest of all the current translations, but I dream of a translation being made one day that lets Paul be himself, rather than his respectable *alter ego*.

Acting it out

Christian drama has all too often been pretty terrible. For some reason Christian drama largely only means one thing: A 'sketch' consisting of a few bad puns (often in jokes) followed up with its one and only point being hit home with the dramatic equivalent of a sledgehammer.

In contrast, most people, inside church as well as outside it, are used to a huge range of dramatic forms such as films, serials, news broadcasts, soap operas, mini-series, musicals, sit-coms and yes, even sketches. It would be great to see Christian drama moving away from the sketch-that-answers-everything which sits as a complete unit. Perhaps we could see short bits of drama that just raise questions rather than answering them. It could be even better if it was followed up by time for the audience/congregation to discuss what they've seen, rather than have 'the answer' given to them by a preacher straight away. Or maybe we could see something serious that had no jokes (using that term loosely). Or we could present something that just gives a snapshot of the real world.

The other major area for acting it out is amongst those who wouldn't consider themselves as the next Robert DeNiro or Nicole Kidman – in fact, people who don't really like acting particularly. Next time you're in a group that's going to be reading a passage, why not take a role each? You could even print it off beforehand in script format so everyone has the same translation and can see when it's their turn. You're not necessarily looking for a sensational acting performance, just something more interesting than the monotone mentioned at the top of the chapter. You can also try it at home, just reading with housemates, wives, children and so on.

Other approaches

There are numerous other ways in which you can approach the Bible. Here's a list with brief explanations to give you the idea:

Meditation on a passage or verse
Either thinking through a passage (seeing what jumps out; what is God saying? etc.) or concentrating more on a particular verse or phrase.

Memorization
There are loads of methods for memorizing passages, such as repeating them over and over; or writing them down and

crossing out a word at a time; or thinking of acronyms, etc. As you do this, Scripture becomes much more part of you and gets ingrained in your memory, so it comes to mind at the relevant time.

Structural encounters
Often the Bible stories have clear structure to them. Work through what is happening at each stage (e.g. Elijah encountering God after the wind, earthquake, fire and small voice). Think through each stage one at a time.

Contemplation
Repeat the same passage over and over again. Gradually the emphasis should shift from the words to the God behind them. Repetitive dance beats might help you do this as well.

General film clips
Are there any clips from films that illustrate, enlighten or reflect a particular passage (or demonstrate the opposite)?

Drama
Plan/write some form of drama based on the passage you are studying. It could be a group drama or a monologue. This works well both for gospel passages and for rhetoric such as the Epistles.

Retelling the story
Work out ways to retell a particular passage. You could be an eyewitness or a journalist, or be writing a letter to a friend. This makes you re-work the story, looking at it from a different angle.

Speaking out in worship
Many parts of the Bible, such as the Psalms, were written to be spoken out in corporate worship. How does it feel to be

using the Bible in this way rather than learning propositional truths?

Sensory exploration
Read a passage and then get hold of things that make the five senses feel the same way as they would have done then. Read Jesus' describing himself as living water when you're hot, sweaty and thirsty. Have a glass of wine whilst reading about the wedding at Cana.

Pictures and maps
To help you get your head around what is going on where, it can be helpful to get hold of a map of the relevant area or building (if there isn't one to hand, try drawing your own). Or you could try to make time-lines or family trees when it all gets a bit complicated. Or just find pictures of how it might have looked, when you read a passage.

Questions for you and your group

- Why do we often find it so difficult to 'get into' the Bible?
- How often do you think we should 'get into' it?
- How easy or difficult is it for you to get into it?
- What's your favourite bit?
- What bits do you not understand?
- Would it be a book you would want on your desert island? Why or why not?
- What has helped you understand its meaning today?

Also see Matt Page's website: http://biblefilms.blogspot.com

29

And Finally . . .

Lee and Baz

Many effective plans have been written on the back of an envelope or beer mat . . .

Grab an envelope or beer mat now. Scribble down three action points that you know you need to act on after reading our book – and keep it handy as you do them!

The young have aspirations that never come to pass,
the old have reminiscences of what never happened.
Saki (1870–1916)

Don't have aspirations or reminiscences of what may or may not have happened – make *them* a reality – by living *in* reality.

Enjoy your journey.

www.leeandbaz.com

Notes

The Three Rs
1. Heard in a stand-up routine on TV.
2. Meic Pearse and Chris Matthews, *We Must Stop Meeting Like This* (Eastbourne: Kingsway, 1999).
3. It has been said that 10 per cent of people you meet won't anyway!
4. See note 3!

Braveheart
5. John Eldredge, *Wild at Heart* (Nashville: Thomas Nelson, 2001).
6. Martin Scott, *Sowing Seeds of Revival* (Lancaster: Sovereign World, 2001).
7. John Eldredge, *Wild at Heart* (Nashville: Thomas Nelson, 2001).
8. Twentieth Century Fox, 1999.
9. From a TV stand-up routine.
10. Woody Allen in *Annie Hall* (1977).
11. *Compass* magazine, Vol. 1, No. 3.

Free Hugs
12. From a talk on Jim Collins's website.
13. www.freehugscampaign.org

And Whatever Did Happen to the Heroes?
14. Henry Miller (1891–1980), American author, taken from proverbia.net
15. Brenda Sanson on www.unb.ca

Never Been Trained!
16. From a TV stand-up routine.
17. From a TV stand-up routine.

'Me, Change? Impossible' – Or is It?
18. From Gordon Dalbey, *Sons of the Father* (Eastbourne: Kingsway, 2002).
19. Flora Whittemore, quoted in www.thinkexist.com
20. Rosanne Cash on www.thinkexist.com
21. Keri Russell on www.thinkexist.com
22. Don't look for Ann Robinson jokes here!
23. People were 'drunk in the Spirit' in the city centre, and as they prayed for strangers walking past, people came to faith and were healed and got a 'free buzz' and 'life readings' (prophecy!).
24. Linda Harding from Kairos was a great help to me in finding this stuff.
25. That is the bit that makes following Jesus unique.
26. It took me being ill for a week to realize this – d'oh!
27. From www.markroques.com

Crying is for Wimps
28. Hogan Hilling, 'Crying can make you a better man', www.fathersnetwork.org
29. Eileen Mayhew, http://www.bestoflovequotes.com/cryingquotes5.htm
30. *Daily Express*, Friday, 22 September 2006.
31. 'The Way We Live Now', questions for Phil Donahue by David Wallis, *New York Times*, 14 April 2002.
32. Although in 2007 he was, at last, seen crying, during his TV show *Top Gear*, after completing an endurance car race. It had been a tough assignment for him and his co-presenters.

The False Divide

33. Roger Ellis and Chris Seaton, *New Celts* (Eastbourne: Kingsway, 1998).

34. No softeners here – read it again!

35. Tom Ehrich, from www.biblicalrecorder.org

36. Roger Ellis and Chris Seaton, *New Celts* (Eastbourne: Kingsway, 1998).

You are Odd!

37. For any politically correct readers, this board was black and the chalk was white, just like now the whiteboard is white – so get over it!

The Career Magnet

38. Twentieth Century Fox, 1999.

39. Roger Ellis and Chris Seaton, *New Celts* (Eastbourne: Kingsway, 1998).

40. David Adam, *Holy Island* ('Pilgrim Guides' series) (Norwich: Canterbury Press, 2007).

Never on a Sunday

41. *African and Caribbean Evangelical Alliance Magazine*, Nov. 1999–Jan. 2000.

Keep On Keeping On

42. No names here – nosey!

43. Martin Scott, *Sowing Seeds of Revival* (Lancaster: Sovereign World, 2001).

44. Steve Chalke in an interview.

Walk the Plank!

45. John Scotland, verbatim quotation from a talk.

46. L. J. Stevens on www.thinkexist.com

47. Andrew Murray, quoted in Leona Frances Choy, *What Great Evangelicals Believed about the Holy Spirit 1850–1930* (Pennsylvania: Christian Publications, 1990).

Adventurous Youth Work

48. Jimmy Savile was a pioneer DJ in the 1960s and a presenter of *Top of the Pops* and *Jim'll Fix It* on BBC TV in the 1970s – the original kids'-dreams-coming-true programme, long before Oprah.
49. I met him again recently and told him. :)
50. Not that I know if there are twelve or not!
51. Read Shane Claiborne's book *The Irresistible Revolution*, if you dare, for more on this and much more.
52. Based on dialogue from the movie, *The Lion, the Witch and the Wardrobe*.

Hide and Seek

53. Rachel Naomi Remen, clinical professor of family and community medicine at the University of California at San Francisco School of Medicine. Taken from www.thinkexist. com
54. Robert McGee, *The Search for Significance* (Rapha Publications, 1990), pp. 63–64.
55. George New and David Cormack, *Why Do I Do That?* (London: Hodder & Stoughton, 1997).

Why I Hate Religion

56. Mark Deobler, head coach of the Grove Church.
57. Philip Yancey, *What's So Amazing About Grace?* (Grand Rapids, MI: Zondervan Publishing House, new edn 2002).

Sorry to Bother You . . .

58. Gil Bailie, verbatim quotation.
59. Referring to Matthew 11:12. There is some confusion over this often-quoted passage, but maybe Jesus borrowed images from his world here, and that made this shocking. Maybe he is speaking here positively of 'spiritual warriors' who were storming or fighting their way into God's kingdom. Maybe I need to learn Greek after all!

60. See Matt Page's chapter, 'Found in Translation', on how to use the Bible as a man!

61. To put this into today's context, we may have to replace the Samaritan with a paedophile or a prostitute.

62. John Eldredge, *Wild at Heart* (Nashville: Thomas Nelson, 2001).

63. John Cleese, TV interview.

Over Ten Years to Walk 350 Miles

64. www.thewayofthespirit.com/about/wigglesworth.aspx

Zany Gob Case

65. From the film *An Inconvenient Truth*.

66. Chinese proverb, taken from www.thinkexist.com

67. Romans 8:26.

68. 2 Corinthians 2.

Reality vs. Fantasy

69. Matthew Fitzgerald, Relationship Correspondent, quoted in www.askmen.com/dating

70. Iris Murdoch, quoted in www.worldofquotes.com

71. Earl Nightingale, quoted in www.quotations.about.com

Found in Translation

72. Hirst won the Turner Prize in 1995 for a piece called *Mother and Child*.

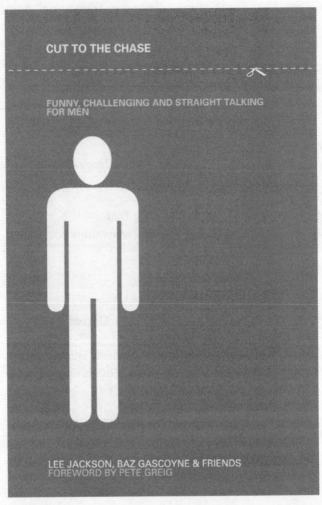

CUT TO THE CHASE

FUNNY, CHALLENGING AND STRAIGHT TALKING
FOR MEN

LEE JACKSON, BAZ GASCOYNE & FRIENDS
FOREWORD BY PETE GREIG

Cut to the Chase encourages men to discover what it mean
to be truly masculine. Packed full of quotes, humou
information and true stories, it's raw, gritty and a breath o
fresh air.

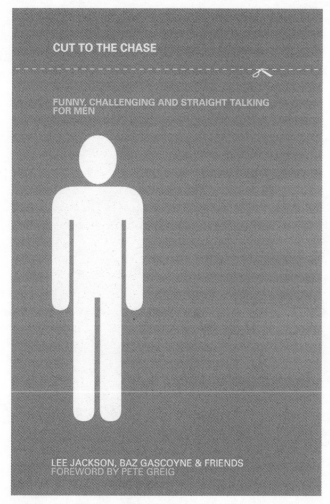

Cut to the Chase Visual Edition is a totally remixed version of
Lee and Baz's groundbreaking men's book *Cut to the Chase*.
With extra content and pioneering design by Lloyd Kinsley, it
brings their best-selling book alive to visual readers, non-
book blokes or to those who just need a quick-reference guide
to being a better bloke in the twenty-first century.